The
PRIVILEGE
of YOUTH

The

PRIVILEGE
of YOUTH

The Inspirational Story of a
Teenager's Search for
Friendship and Acceptance

DAVE PELZER

MICHAEL JOSEPH
an imprint of
PENGUIN BOOKS

MICHAEL JOSEPH

Published by the Penguin Group

Penguin Books Ltd, 80 Strand, London WC2R 0RL, England

Penguin Group (USA), Inc., 375 Hudson Street, New York, New York 10014, USA

Penguin Books Australia Ltd, 250 Camberwell Road, Camberwell, Victoria 3124, Australia

Penguin Books Canada Ltd, 10 Alcorn Avenue, Toronto, Ontario, Canada M4V 3B2

Penguin Books India (P) Ltd, 11 Community Centre, Panchsheel Park, New Delhi - 110 017, India

Penguin Books (NZ) Ltd, Cnr Rosedale and Airborne Roads, Albany, Auckland, New Zealand

Penguin Books (South Africa) (Pty) Ltd, 24 Sturdee Avenue, Rosebank 2196, South Africa

Penguin Books Ltd, Registered Offices: 80 Strand, London WC2R 0RL, England

www.penguin.com

Published in the United States of America by Dutton 2004
Published simultaneously in Great Britain by Michael Joseph 2004

1

Printed in Great Britain by Clays Ltd, St Ives plc

A CIP catalogue record for this book is available from the British Library

HB ISBN 0-718-14668-9
TPB ISBN 0-718-14669-7

DEDICATION

As always, without my lovely wife, Marsha; my incredible son, Stephen; and God, I am nothing. I have been blessed by their love and encouragement. My family sacrifices so much to allow me to do the work I do. I am grateful beyond words for giving me such a wonderful life.

This book is also dedicated with deepest sincerity to:

David Howard and Paul Brazell, life-long friends and brothers-in-arms in the promotion of unimaginable chaos in our search for days of adventure that we prayed would never end.

Mr. Dan Brazell, the father I never had. Not a day goes by that I do not think of you. I've passed many of the life lessons you've taught me on to my son.

Michael A. Marsh, truly one of the most extraordinary individuals I have ever known, whose vast knowledge, guidance, and love literally changed to course of my life. Thanks, Sarge.

Mrs. Beth Ann Brazell and daughter Dori, for putting up

with me and allowing me a glimpse into your loving family.

Sandy Marsh, the sweetest lady I know, for your gentle guidance and everlasting inspiration.

The Marsh Boys: William and "Moonraker" Eric, thank you both for all the years of love. Both of you made me laugh when my heart cried for the brothers I missed so much.

Mrs. Jacqueline Howard and daughter Sheryl, for treating me as one of your own. "Mrs. H," you've always been one classy dame. Thanks for everything, "Mom"!

John and Linda Walsh, thank you allowing me into your foster home and introducing me to the wonderful world of Duinsmoore.

The Neyland Family, Mr. and Mrs. Jolly, and anyone else within the confines of Suburban Park, for tolerance, patience, and forgiveness. I meant no harm.

The tolerant and even saintly men and women of the Menlo Park Police Department, especially Detective Joe Ochella. I've learned my lesson now: fight for truth, honor, and lower speed limits with fewer automotive shenanigans.

And finally, to Ronald, Stan, Russell, and Kevin: good men, all, who too endured and made their lives all the better.

CONTENTS

CONTENTS

The
PRIVILEGE
of YOUTH

1

❧

A Good Man's Departure

April 21, 1999, 2:35 A.M.—It's been a long four days. In the last ninety-six hours I've crisscrossed the country, traveling to five states, and have only been able to steal seven hours of sleep. I pride myself on a strong work ethic, but now my body is on the verge of collapse. What began as a slight quiver last week has now become an uncontrollable seizure of my right hand. I've been able to hide it in public by casually placing one hand on top of the other or making a tight fist behind my back until the tremors pass. But now in the nearly freezing weather of Northern Ohio, for the life of me I cannot steady my hand so I can insert the stupid key into the doorknob of my motel room. After three attempts my patience erodes to the point that I begin mumbling a string of off-color language to the howling wind. Huffing, I slide off my computer case, which contains my hefty laptop, and my worn overstuffed satchel from my left shoulder. Steadying myself, my left hand gently clutches my right one just below the wrist and, after another few stabs with the gold-colored key, I'm finally able to fling open the door to my humble room.

I've been on the road for twenty-one days, with another twenty-three days to go before I can catch a glimmer of my fiancée's face, capture the fragrance from her long auburn hair, let alone hold her by my side in the middle of the night. Looking up at the darkened sky I search to find the North Star, knowing that my teenage son, Stephen, is somewhere on the other side of the country in the middle of a deep slumber. He's about to begin baseball season. How I love to watch that boy play. I can visualize the countless times Stephen would be up at bat, and how I would stand behind the batting cage as if I were him, a child, living an endless stream of days filled with wonder. I'd dissect the grip on Stephen's blue-colored bat and how he would twirl it in the air like a helicopter, his body positioned to hit, and the way he'd shake his little butt. I'd always burst with excitement whenever I heard the distinctive crack from the bat as the baseball sailed deep into the lush green field. I never really had the chance to play baseball as a kid. My thoughts begin to escape me, but I instantly slam that door shut. The intensity of my career coupled with my self-imposed mental compartmentalization is protection for me. I do so by remaining rigidly focused when out on the road. I know from past brief lapses that if I let down my guard for even a few moments, I will cry a river of tears from missing those I love. I also place a great deal of responsibility on myself that borders at times on anxiety—worrying about oversleeping or missing a flight, driving hundreds of miles in the middle of the night with bewildering, mind-numbing directions, or my biggest fear of not "being there" and not giving my absolute best to so many folks who invite me into their communities and organizations.

April is Child Abuse Prevention Awareness month and I dedicate myself to this cause by traveling from one end of the country to the other, working with teens and adults to help them focus on harvesting their inner strength to overcome a horrendous past, praising those who protect and work with those at risk, and providing all-day workshops on the psychology and resilience of this subject. Today my day began at three in the morning, taping a few radio interviews over the phone, before studying for my eight-hour workshop. Then with the program completed, books signed, and encouragement offered to those struggling with difficult situations, I raced to the airport, completely exhausted, changed clothes in the confines of the airport bathroom stall, and hopped on a plane, arriving just in time to speak at a fund-raiser for a local Boys & Girls club, before catching my final flight of the day in order to start all over again and drive somewhere in the middle of Northern Ohio. As always, when my adrenaline fades it's instantly replaced with a crushing force of exhaustion. At least now, whenever I make my midnight trek, I have sense enough to drive with the air conditioner on, the windows rolled down, and the voice of a local radio talk show host ranting at full volume. Being on the road over two hundred days a year, I have an intense fear of falling asleep behind the wheel . . . again. The last time I nodded off, God must have been watching over me. At full speed and with me dead to the world my rental car crossed the median. I awoke just in time to gaze up at what looked like a pair of headlights belonging to some gigantic UFO about to make contact with my car. Through sheer luck and stupidity, I mashed down on the accelerator, missing the semi truck just enough that the car shook from its wake, while I emptied my lungs chanting, "Oh my God! Oh my God! Oh my God!"

Before closing the door of my room, I look at the car and smile. After heaving my two mammoth-sized travel bags on the bed, I survey my home for the next few hours: a clean, pine-scented setting, a small worn bed, a fresh set of towels, and a phone. I can't ask for anything more, except for a working heater . . . which refuses to do anything but pump in air that is somehow colder than outside. I'm too tired to care so I simply give up. Anyway, I tell myself that by the time the room warms up, I would have already taken a quick nap, showered, shaved, repacked, and would be on my way to work. After unpacking, I sit on the edge of the bed then notice the telephone's blinking orange light. I figure it's probably my sponsor, who's being courteous, to invite me out to dinner.

Dinner. Food. Sleep. For me these are *luxuries* I can rarely afford. I am always in a frantic state whenever I speak in front of an audience, to the point that I cannot keep anything down. I try to hide my fear, but there have been occasions when my clients who set up the programs can see my apprehension that sometimes brims to the surface. Then, when I fly out again, for some reason my stomach is still in knots. The only solution: I rarely eat. At least yesterday I was able to gulp down some o.j. between my two morning radio shows. Only after I am through for the day, which can be late into the evening, do I reward myself by roaming through the empty streets, searching for a bite to eat. On rare occasions I actually indulge myself with a real sit-down dinner. And when I do, I savor every bite of every morsel. For me, hunger is another switch I'm able to turn off at will. It's a trick I learned many, many years ago.

I know in my heart that I have the most honorable motives for my oddities. I have a revolting past that at times still terrifies me to the core. But yet every day I have to crawl back into the darkest recesses of my former life for the sole purpose of qualifying my message. I usually need to "go there" three, four, five times a day, or more, pouring out my soul, exposing every fiber of my being, in the vain hope of encouraging and praising others. Since the birth of my son, I woke up to some of the atrocities around me and decided to make a difference, as so many other individuals did for me years ago. Those two primary reasons are why I push myself. If it wasn't for the invaluable assistance of others, I was destined to be doomed.

With the two fluffed pillows I jammed behind my lower back, I snatch a file and scrutinize every piece of information I can digest for today's first program. I pride myself on knowing my presentation backward and forward yet being completely spontaneous, so I can give the program without the aid of a single note. I make a quick mental note

that my day will begin with my first radio interview—
which is less than two hours from now—and my last program will probably end somewhere around nine, nine-thirty
tonight . . . which means I'll most likely crawl back to my
motel room around eleven-thirty. I'm thankful I won't have
to drive somewhere else in the middle of the night. At least
tomorrow, *tonight,* my mind corrects, I can get some sleep,
grab a Big Mac, and pray that my boxer shorts and my
socks that I'll soon wash in the sink will be completely dry
before I carefully and painstakingly repack every article in
its place; assurance that I'll be able to carry my necessities
for the next round of flights.

After studying my folder and going over the exact sequence of what to speak on, I allow myself the pleasure of
flipping on the news on television. Since Stephen and I love
the same baseball team, catching an update allows me a
chance of being just a little closer to my son. Because I have
little trust in the ancient alarm clock or the clerk at the reg-
istration desk who looks like she can slip into a coma at any
minute, I set my mental clock to wake me up in just under
ninety minutes, which is more than enough time for me to
recharge my batteries and give the day every ounce of myself. Before dozing off I clasp my hands together and mumble through my prayers. Although I desperately miss my
family and push myself to extremes, I do love my life and
all it entails.

Slipping away I feel the tension ease throughout the
length of my body. I catch a final glimpse of the television
and decide I'm too lazy to switch it off. I let go of my right

hand as the shaking subsides. My mind plays a mental tape of children running in the sunshine with their hands raised in the air as if playing a game of cops and robbers. My dream tells me it must be a serious game, since no one is laughing. From somewhere a dull ring penetrates my dream. I think it's part of my dream and try to ignore the sound, but the ringing continues to become louder and sharper until I bolt upright in the bed thinking I somehow overslept and committed my own cardinal sin of being late. But the alarm clock reads just after three in the morning. I've only been asleep for about eight minutes. Though the ringing from the telephone continues, I become entranced by the television set displaying my dream. I can't seem to understand why children are being marched outside in single file with their hands thrust in the air while an army of police officers have seemingly quarantined the entire area. The commentator dispels my ignorance. *"Oh my God!"* I whisper. *"I can't believe it!"*

As I shake my head, denying the tragedy in front of my eyes, I stretch to grab the phone. Before I can place the receiver to my ear, the voice of my fiancée, Marsha, screams, "Thank God! I've been trying to reach you! Have you heard?" Marsha, a lady of absolute grace, who directs the entire operation of our frantic, hypersonic-speed office, and who keeps everything under control, is now on the verge of panic. "Where have you been?! I've been trying to reach you. . . . Have you heard?"

Turning back to the catastrophe in front of me, I nod my head up and down. Still mesmerized by the television, with every ounce of my being depleted, I reply in stoic short sentences. "Um, sorry. My cell-phone battery ran down. I just came in a few minutes ago. I didn't want to call you and wake you up. . . . Yeah, I'm seeing it on TV now. My God, I . . . I can't believe it. . . . How could this have happened?"

"No, it's not that! I'm not calling about the shooting. . . ." Her voice then softens to a whisper. "You don't know. You haven't heard?" I can hear the pace of Marsha's breathing pick up. "Are you sitting down?"

My heart jumps to marathon speed. My vision is suddenly clear and my mind wide awake. The receiver of my phone strikes the side of my head from my trembling hand. I think it, but can't form the words. Shutting my eyes, my worst nightmare has come true. With perfect clarity, I picture Stephen's bright eyes and wide smile.

One step ahead of my terror Marsha calmly states, "It's not Stephen. Stephen's fine. He's okay. And I know you're exhausted, so please, just tell me you're sitting down." My brain now tallies a long list starting with my oldest brother, Ron, whom I haven't seen or spoken to directly in over eight years. I fear that Ron, a police officer of over twenty years, had been shot in the line of duty. My first thought is to throw everything into the rental car and race back to the airport, catching the first flight to . . .

"Dave," Marsha interrupts, "Dan Brazell passed away."

With my free hand I pound my knee as I slowly rock back and forth on the side of the bed. ". . . should have known. I should have known. It's not like it's my first time with this . . . I . . . I should have . . . have known."

"I'm so sorry," Marsha cries. "Dan, he was like a father to you, wasn't he?"

"Yeah," I choke up. "Dan's the kind of father any kid would have wanted for a dad."

"Was he that sick?"

"No! He was sick, yeah, but, uhh, last time I saw Dan, um . . . was the day he went to the doctor to get a clean bill of health. At least that's what he told me when I called later that day. I can't believe it. I just saw Dan right before Christmas. He looked, fine, so good. . . ." As my voice rambled on, I kept repeating in my mind that it seemed only yesterday that I had just seen him.

Within minutes Marsha eased me back to normalcy. I almost had a clean getaway but, before saying good-bye, I fibbed that I was getting enough sleep and eating well. Marsha worries about me and constantly lectures me on taking care of myself. After hanging up the phone with Marsha, I dialed one of the only telephone numbers I knew by heart since I was a young teen: the Brazell family. I left a brief message, replaced the phone in its cradle, then lay back on the bed while listening to the howling wind as it seeped through the gaps in the wall of my motel room. Closing my eyes I could see the man who, in an odd sense, had played the role of my father since the days I was a frightened and, at times, manic teenager in foster care. The same man who guided me into adulthood, and who years later held my own son, Stephen, in his mighty arms.

Due to my frantic lifestyle and my own home being hours away from his, I never had the chance to see Dan as much as I wanted to. Our last encounter almost never happened. After leaving my two-bedroom condominium at three in the morning in order to make the drive down to the San Francisco Bay Area to have my unique sports car serviced by the dealer—who claimed they needed the vehicle all day—I was surprised when the maintenance was completed hours earlier. When I phoned Dan, he seemed reluctant to see me. Baiting him, I told Dan I had something to show him. The last time I said something like that to him I was eighteen and showed up in the neighborhood in a brand-new Corvette that the car dealership I had worked for loaned me for becoming salesman of the month.

The first thing I noticed about Dan when I saw him was how tired and thinner he looked since our last visit. But his smile for me never waned. In his home, where we had spent so many hours together when I was a teenager, I excitedly ran down the "what I've been up to" checklist that ranged from my son's progress in school, my upcoming marriage to Marsha, and my career as an author and presenter that, after being mismanaged and surviving off of Cup-a-Soups and French bread for years, had recently taken off. I was shocked when Mr. Brazell casually informed me that he had had a bout with cancer. I felt like a complete idiot rambling on about Dave this, Dave that. Dave, Dave, Dave. For years, because of my low self-esteem, I had the tendency to try and overimpress without really meaning to. Especially when it came to Dan.

As I was spilling over with apologies, Dan and his wife, Beth, just smiled. Making it no big deal, Dan assured me he had a clean bill of health. More than anyone else in my life, Dan knew how much I hated that disease. It was Dan that I fled to when my biological father had died in my arms from cancer. Then, years later, one of my foster fathers, a man of great courage, became stricken by the same illness. The word itself summoned such dread for me.

Strolling outside with his arm around my shoulder, Dan again assured me that he was in the best of health. In fact he and his wife were about to leave for another semiannual checkup.

"So, this is it?!" Dan exclaimed, as we approached my black sports car. "Who would have thought . . . the terror of Duinsmoore. . . ."

For Dan and me it wasn't about the fancy car or the overrated success of a few books I had written. Stopping in front of the Lotus Esprit sports car, we both took in the moment and nodded our heads. I bent down to Dan's ear and whispered, "You." Dan turned back up to me and smiled. "You knew," I stated. "You always treated me like a real person and kicked me in the behind when I needed it. You really cared about me and I can't tell you how much that still means to me. This block was the neighborhood I loved and you were the father I never had but always prayed for."

"Well," Dan said, brushing it off, "you overcame a lot. You did it yourself. And, if we, the neighborhood did anything, well, we just put you on course. You had to carry the load. You drove us crazy. . . . You had this entire block in an uproar. . . ."

11

"Privilege of youth, Dan. Privilege of youth," I grinned.

"And now *you're* the one helping kids," Dan said with a smile.

"Duty, honor, and country," I joked. "Truth, justice, and the American way!"

Strolling around the car, the smile I had known within Dan's eyes for years still shined through. The man who had engineered and rebuilt so many cars by hand, rubbed the sides of the Lotus as if it were a piece of art. As Dan slid into the tiny driver's seat and turned over the engine, he seemed like a teenager. While he tapped the accelerator, I sensed how much Dan wanted to take the car out for a quick spin. Fantasizing, I imagined Dan behind the steering wheel with me beside him, tearing down the road at hypersonic speed without a care in the world.

Dan gave me another nod. "Take it. . . ." I mouthed to him. "Go ahead, take it for a spin." For a second, Dan's left hand gripped the steering wheel and the other on the stick shift. An eternity passed within a few beats of time. But I knew I was making Dan late for his doctor's appointment. With Beth standing beside Dan as he crawled out, I knew it was time to leave.

We stood next to each other, slightly nodding our heads before embracing. I always hated saying good-bye to him. "I know I say this all the time, but I love you. I love you, Dad . . . Dan . . ." I slipped.

"You're a good son, David." Dan hugged back.

Sliding into the car, and while adjusting my sunglasses, I proclaimed, "Next time, we take her out for a spin."

Dan nodded in approval. Then, playing the never ending role as the concerned father, he inquired, "Ever get any tickets?"

Taking in the scene, I let out a laugh. I was seventeen again, wide-eyed, and spilling over with adventure. Raising my eyebrows, I confessed, "Not me, Sir. I'm a *good* boy!"

Minutes later at the end of the block, I eased the black, needle-nose Lotus beside Dan and Beth's car before we both drove off in opposite directions. I had thought of making a grand departure of racing through the gears, but reminded myself I was a grown adult, in my mid-thirties, and therefore too old, and far too mature, for such a childlike spurt of recklessness. So, I waved good-bye and casually headed northbound on Bay Road. When their car disappeared behind my rearview mirror, a sudden impulse took over. I slammed the car to a stop and, as I had years before on the same street, my mind ran through a simple but thorough checklist: (1) Check for police, (2) Ensure there are no children or any other pedestrians in the street, (3) Make certain there is adequate clearance in front of the driver at all times, and (4) Reverify checklist and think about what you're about to get yourself into. Two-point-four seconds later, I took a deep breath, leaned back into the seat, floored the accelerator, popped the clutch, and sped through the gears.

With a streak of burnt rubber and grayish-black smoke in my wake, I quietly announced, "Adios, Dan. See ya next time."

* * *

And now, in the middle of the night, thousands of miles away, in the midst of a freezing room, I sat on the edge of the bed. I didn't cry. And for a moment my trembling hand seemed to subside. With my fingers on my forehead and with my eyes closed, all I could do was listen to the howling wind and realize how much Dan Brazell and that small neighborhood changed the course of my life.

2

❧

A Lost Boy

Years before I met Dan Brazell or those who lived on
Duinsmoore Way, I endured a miserable childhood. As long
as I could remember, since I was a small boy, I always felt
unworthy. An unwanted outsider. For the life of me, I could
not do anything that was remotely acceptable for my mother.
I always seemed to be in some sort of trouble. And as much
as I tried to amaze or fought hard to impress that I was not
simpleminded or tried to prove my worthiness, my existence only became more dark and sinister. With every day,
all I wanted, all I craved, was to simply belong.

One morning at school, out of the blue, my teachers re-
ported my condition to the authorities. It took twelve years,
but I was finally liberated. I was placed into foster care. Finally, I belonged. I was somebody. I was no longer an animal
existing in a darkened basement/garage, but a real person.
For no apparent reason I had surmised that the words "foster child" were a unique distinction of honor. Not some
everyday kid from "Normal Town" USA, but a *Foster Kid*. A

kid that had endured some misfortune and now caught a lucky break.

It took a while, but I caught on that being a foster kid was not as I dreamt it to be. Nearly a year later, barely in my teens, I had lived in four separate foster homes. Besides coming to terms with my past, it seemed I never truly had a chance to adjust to my everyday environment, then once I got a foothold, I was suddenly ousted to another surrounding.

After spending part of my summer with one family, I felt convinced I now had a chance of settling down. I couldn't wait for my first day of junior high. When the big day arrived, I proudly showed up at my new school in fresh corduroy pants, brown Hush Puppies shoes, and my new black-framed glasses. I was proud that I was carrying a lunch box to school. Standing in the hallway, I marveled at the shiny blue school lockers, and how enormous the upper grade students were—until I discovered that they were in the same grade as I, and I was probably the smallest kid in the entire school.

During my first period, homeroom class, the entire class sat on tall wooden stools. I was proud that I sat among the tallest boys, who seemed to know everyone. With a quick series of wide smiles from the group, I felt I was accepted as one of their own. When the group mocked the teacher whenever he spoke, I, too, snickered at their jokes. As the boys teased our teacher, ever so slowly, without anyone catching on, rather than sitting hunched over in my usual reclusive pose, I began to sit up perfectly straight. With my shoulders arched back, I stared at the boys from my table, who suddenly bowed their heads, whispering something that I thought was about our teacher's receding hairline.

One of them commented on how much one girl from across the table had grown during the summer. Glancing over, she didn't seem that tall to me. At the time, I had always thought that girls were exactly the same as boys; with the exception that they had squeakier voices, longer hair, and some wore makeup and had bumps on their chest.

The more the boys leaned over and leered at the girl, the more I envied to be part of their inner circle. When they broke out in laughter, I, too, howled even though I had no idea what anyone had said. Then, in an instant, the group stopped, raised their heads in unison, and scowled at me. One of the boys turned to me and said, "Hey, Tiny Tim, where'd you get your threads, the Salvation Army?"

Growing up and throughout my time in foster care, I'd stutter whenever I became nervous or embarrassed, so I now fought to keep my responses short. "Nope," I proudly announced, "Kmart."

"Man," one of the boys blurted, "what a spaz!"

Feeling a quick retort was required, I extended my right arm and countered, "Nope, not me. Look, I ain't got no twitches."

The table became quiet until another kid, who seemed sincere, asked, "You're new here, aren't you, kid?"

I shook my head yes.

"So, you don't know anybody, do ya?"

Thinking for a moment I answered, "Nope . . . 'cept just you guys."

"Lucky for you," the trustworthy one stated. "Anyway . . . you see that girl over there?"

Wanting to prove I wasn't slow, I swiveled my head, adjusted my glasses, then squinted my eyes to sharpen my look. "Which one?"

From behind my back a small chorus of laughter erupted. I thought for sure the group of boys were impressed with my lightninglike response. After a few seconds of no guidance, I thrust my finger at the likely candidate. "That one?" I whispered.

"Nope," the kid with the attitude snickered.

"That one?" I pointed at another girl.

"No, not *her*," one of the boys howled.

Growing frustrated I jabbed my finger at another girl only to receive the same response. In the back of my mind I began to sense that I was probably being set up for some catastrophe, but, I told myself, this was junior high and big kids wouldn't do anything like that. Besides, I continued, I knew I was in too deep to retreat back to my inner shell, for the majority of the class was beginning to stare in my direction. I thought about lowering my hand and hiding it underneath the table. Before I could, one of the boys grabbed it and hissed, "Over there. *That* girl!"

Regaining my "wanna be just like one of the guys" composure, I extended the length of my arm and thrust my finger blurting, "*That* one?"

The entire group smiled as they nodded their heads in

agreement. I kept my head down as I listened to one of my new friends say, "She thinks you're cute."

"Nah," I gushed. I never had a girl like *me* before. "Not me."

"Really, man," a different voice stated. "I can tell. She keeps lookin' at your shoes."

With my mind spinning a million miles a minute, before I could utter a reply, another kid, the one who had teased me about my attire, chimed, "Definitely the shoes! Chicks dig shoes. And I oughta know!" The other boys again gestured in agreement.

A different boy said, "Listen to him, little man, he's been to first base."

"*Second* base!" the boy corrected.

"No way!?" another boy exclaimed.

"Way!" the first boy stated, shaking his head as the other boy's eyes grew wide.

Everything seemed to fly over my head. All I could do was turn and gaze at the young lady with my mouth hung open. She had shoulder-length blond hair that shined at the ends, blindingly white teeth, and she wore a shiny floral dress. After her eyes scanned me, her cheeks blushed. Covering her mouth, the girl giggled something to her girl-friends at her table.

Turning my attention back to the boys, who seemed bunched together, I raised my shoulders. "I don't get it," I confessed.

"Man," one of them announced, "she wants you."

"For what?" I fired back, beginning to feel apprehensive.

"You know . . . she wants to do it with you," one answered while slowly nodding his head until other boys motioned as well.

Without thinking, without understanding, I became caught up in the moment and gestured as well. "So, what do I do?" I asked.

The athletic, "first base" boy jumped in. "What you do is, if you really want to impress a fox like that is, you compliment them. You call 'em a horror."

"A *horror?*" I questioned.

"Yep," the boys all nodded. "Chicks dig it."

"Hmm," I said, letting on to the cool guys that I was thinking of how I was going to make my move. Even though I was new to the world of girls, I had sat in the back of the movie theater, watching the latest James Bond film *Live and Let Die* dozens upon dozens of time, so I felt I could come up with a smooth line just like my action hero.

Without any prodding from the group, with little hesitation or scant idea of what I was going to say, I leaned over to the girl's table, adjusted my glasses before placing my elbow on my knee, then in a sudden nervous, raspy voice, I looked into the girl's eyes, swallowed hard, and announced, "Hi. . . . You are the prettiest-looking horror I've ever seen."

The entire table of ladies gasped while they covered their mouths. Their eyes grew wide from what I thought was my first-rate salutation. Ol' 007 would have been proud. But a split second later the room became as quiet as a church. Paralyzing seconds passed. I smiled at the girl, who jerked her head away from me. It was then that I knew

20

something was wrong. Turning back to the group of boys, I heard, "Man, I can't believe you did that." The others, as usual, nodded in agreement.

My throat began to tighten as my frustration grew. I could not figure out what I had said that was so wrong. I had thought the word *horror* meant that the girl was so pretty she was scary. Just like she's so *hot*. Or the expression *dig it*, or when other kids would say a girl was *foxy*. I didn't always get it, but I believed they were words that the cool kids said as part of their language.

With my mind spinning again, I could not come to a simple black-and-white solution. As my throat began to ease from its tightness, I stuttered in a tone louder than desired, "I don't . . . I don't get it! All I did was . . . was call . . . 'er a *horror!*"

I then had the undivided attention of every single being. Even the teacher spun around, studied his pupils, and announced, "Good. I'm glad to see you all finally paying attention."

Feeling everyone's gaze on me, I closed my eyes, hunched my shoulders, and clenched my jittery hands under the table.

"Oh, dude," one of the boys stated, "you are so toasted."

With my chin buried in my chest, I asked, "Toast?"

When I felt enough seconds had ticked away, I looked up at the boys at the table. In perfect unison, they all murmured, "Kong. Kong. Kong."

All I could do was force a smile. "Kong?"

In less than a minute, the entire class rapped their hands on their tables, chanting in a low voice, "Kong! Kong! Kong!"

This was not good.

For the remainder of the class, I kept my head down and nearly rubbed the skin off my hands. An eternity later when the bell finally rang, I made sure I was the last kid to leave. This was my mistake.

As I approached the door, my senses became keen. I caught a whiff of freshly cut grass. The sun pierced through the morning fog and made everything shine bright. For a second I thought I heard the chirping of a bird. For a few moments I had filed away what a jerk I had made out of myself. When I got home today, I told myself, I would definitely question my foster mother about the slang meaning for the word *horror*.

A half step later an eclipse blocked all light, sound, and my path. I slowly raised my chin until my muscles in my neck ached. In front of me a tree trunk of a boy displayed a hand bigger than my chest. Amazed at his size, all I could do was blink in wonder. Mesmerized, as he leaned toward me, I half stepped forward, helping him to grab the lapel from my shirt. As he breathed like a rabid dog, the corners of my mouth began to dry.

"What'd you say in class?" the boy bellowed.

I had sense enough to understand the tree-trunk boy was the infamous "Kong." The idea of James Bond–like karate chops wouldn't prevail since I neither had the skill nor a stepladder to pummel my opponent. Maybe, I fantasized, I could reason with him. I thought of raising a finger, saying, "I'm glad you asked. How considerate of you. It's simply a small misunderstanding, my good man."

Yet, with my mouth now completely dry, all I could do was swallow as I turned my head away, saying in the lowest voice possible, *"Horror?"*

A second later tiny bright silver stars danced in front of my eyes. Kong was so quick that I didn't see his hand move. "I says, 'What'd you call my sister?' "

My lopsided brain searched for an answer, anything but *that* word. I raised my shoulder as if to tell Kong I didn't understand. "What's the word?" he asked. "Come on, give it to me!"

I braced myself, closed my eyes and gently responded, *"Horror? . . ."*

Another flash and stars again filled my vision. With blood seeping from my mouth and nose, Kong readied his cocked arm, asking the same question. With my mind lost in a fog, I kept thinking there must be an echo somewhere, for the rhythm of *horror* hit, *horror* smash, *horror* pummel continued until after more than a dozen poundings, gorilla-boy, King Kong, pounded his chest in front of the crowd, bellowing, "Man, don't you ever, ever call my sister a *whore* again!"

With Kong's departure a small circle of kids surveyed the damage. I felt they were vultures surveying fresh roadkill. All I could do was turn my back and, with my fingers stretched out for my glasses, on my hands and knees I found them, while scrambling to pick up my scattered school supplies. Another kid almost as small as me bent down to help me. "I see you met the Kongster."

Hesitating, for fear of saying the wrong thing, I nodded my head.

"Don't sweat it. Everybody, well, most everybody, gets a pounding. Don't worry, Kong's a simian. Literally. As dumb as a primate. He's supposed to be in high school, but he flunked out last year." As the boy stood up to leave, he gave me a final warning. "Keep your head down and your mouth shut. They say Kong bites the heads off of live rats and his best friend's a pit bull."

Before I could smile a thank-you, the boy scurried away like a small fish swimming away before the bigger ones glided by to take a bite out of him as well.

As I fled to find a bathroom, various glees broke out from behind me. "Excellent! Man, did you see that? That dude got creamed!" exclaimed one boy. "Unbelievable! That was just too much!" hollered another. But the one that sank into the back of my mind was, "Man, this is gonna be a hell of a year. Welcome to junior high, geekster!"

My first day of my new life, in a new school, I ended up with a bloody nose, two black eyes, a swollen, cut lip, broken glasses, and not an ounce of dignity. And in its stead: a thirst to discover the true meaning of the word *whore*.

The next few months of my life became a whirlwind of moving to several different foster homes throughout the county, only to end up being "placed" with the same family that I started off with and returning to the same school where I had been the object of torment. For some reason, since I had trouble remembering all the different homes, names, addresses, and telephone numbers, I had stupidly assumed I would somehow be granted a fresh start in my former school. But it only took a matter of hours for word to spread that the small-fry, fish-eyed, lens-wearing "geekster" had returned.

Every day I programmed myself to keep my head down and my mouth shut. I realized there were different cliques of kids—the tough boys sporting black vinyl jackets, the cool kids with their BMX bikes, the sport jocks, the kids with brains, the makeup queens with strawberry lip gloss and tiny tube-tops, and the seemingly perfect china doll–like girls strutting in Jordache hip-hugger pants and rabbit-fur jackets. Passing through the hallways as others lined up to get to their next class, I felt lucky if one of the roaming sharks didn't find me.

For the most part, even when I kept to myself, my predators would locate me. I was picked on at the bus stop before school, during school recess, on the bus after school; or whenever I'd skip the bus to avoid confrontation, I was jumped on the walk home. As before when I lived at my mother's house, I never fought back, never raised a hand, or possessed the common sense to run away. I took my licks until the bullies grew tired, the chants from the crowds subsided, or my assailants took pity on me. As much as I wanted to strike back with superhuman force, I knew I had the defensive capabilities of a scarecrow.

My main obstacle wasn't my slim frame, my lack of fashion sense, or being the new kid, but my *overbearing mouth*. A majority of the time I had the perfect timing of always stating the wrong things at the wrong times. To compound matters, whenever my nervous adrenaline flowed, my brain whirled a million miles a second for the exact things to say, while my mouth would either hang open or stutter to form a few words.

Desperate to fit in and be one of the kids, one weekend I spent my time clinging to my high school–age foster sisters, who strutted to the nearby mall while stopping to cake on mounds of makeup just to *be seen* and *hang out*. I couldn't understand why they acted one way at the shopping center and another way when under the watchful eyes of our foster parents. Either way, I thought they were the prettiest, most self-assured ladies I knew. In order to tag along with my foster sisters, the deal was that as soon as we entered the mall, I was to make myself scarce and under no circumstances approach them. From across the second floor of the open divide, I stared in wonder as the girls smacked on their gum and seemed to giggle every few seconds after some boy would say something. But what amazed me the most was their exaggerated hand gestures and how they twirled the ends of their hair with the tips of their fingers.

That weekend a revelation came to me. I figured out that it wasn't exactly *what* one said, but rather *how* one said it. All I did was replay in my mind everything my older foster sisters did at the mall. I stood in front of my glazed mirror and practiced every nuance the girls employed. Now, I told myself, I was ready to go out and fit in! The next Monday morning, before school started, I wasn't even fazed when one of the bullies and his cluster stopped me in the hallway.

This, I smiled inside, was my moment.

"Hey, Pa . . . Pa . . . Pelzer. . . . What'd you da . . . da . . . do this weekend?"

With hours of rehearsal under my belt and pronouncing every word and copying every small gesture, I took a half step forward, placed both hands on my hips, tossed my shoulder-length shaggy hair to the side, and in a cocky *I could care less attitude* I smacked my lips before saying, "Well, as if it matters, if you must know, I hung out at the mall talking to guys, with my fos . . ."

Before I could finish my sentence, the new Dave Pelzer shocked the group to the point where every single one of the thugs became paralyzed. Now, it was their mouths that hung open. With my hands still glued to my hips, I took another half step forward while giving the bully a wide smile, knowing I got the best of him, until a member of his gang thrust his fist at me, shouting at the top of his lungs, "Oh my God, Tony! Pelzer's queer. He's queer!"

As if waking up from a trance, the chief bully, Tony, seized my collar, threw me to the concrete, and commenced to pound me, much to the delight of half the school. After several blows to the face, Tony stopped, huffing, "Tell me, are you queer? Come on, tell me, are you queer or what?"

Having no idea what Tony's true meaning of another slang word was, and with my brain stuck in neutral, all I could do was sputter, "I guess so. I, I ah, I mean, you guys tell me all the time, how different I am."

The pounding resumed. In between the hits, Tony roared, "Are you gay?"

27

Gay? my pulsating mind screamed. Gay! That was one word I knew the actual meaning of. Having read sections of one of my foster parents' Bible and having been a closet bookworm for years, *gay,* was one of the most upbeat words I knew!

"Answer me, dweeb!" Tony yelled. "Are you gay, or what?"

Between blows, with my hands covering my face, I blared, "Not at the moment. . . . And *you* could stand to be more happy yourself!"

Stupefied, Tony immediately dropped me to the floor. Standing over me, he wasn't sure how to respond until one of Tony's buddies slapped him on the back, warning, "You better go wash your hands, dude; you don't want none of that to rub off on you. The dude's homo!"

Later that afternoon, I limped into my foster sister Nancy's room, with my hands on my hips, begging her to tell me the slang meaning of the words from school. Nancy shook her head in disbelief at my sudden stance and my extreme gullibility. After explaining to me the subtle differences between the boys and girls, she informed me it wouldn't hurt for me "toughen up" a bit. Per Nancy's recommendation, the next weekend I purchased a ticket to a Kurt Russell Disney film, but boldly snuck into an R-rated movie instead. In the darkness, my mouth hung open; this time not from the suave British secret agent but the pulsating heavy bass sounds and the gritty no-nonsense character of Detective Harry Callahan. After sitting through three consecutive showings, I spent the rest of the weekend standing in front of the same mirror as before; but this time, rather than twisting the ends of my hair, I squinted my right eye while tilting my chin ever so slightly, and coldly speaking as if I had gravel in my mouth, asking my reflection, "Do you feel lucky? Well do ya, *punk*?"

The following Monday at school as I closed my locker, Tony and his band of boys appeared, "Hey, Pa . . . Pa . . . Pelzer, I hear you been shoppin' for girls' underwear. Are you wearin' some now?!"

Even though my stomach was in knots and Tony was at least a foot taller and twenty-five pounds heavier than me, I maintained my cool facade. This time, I told myself, I was ready for them. This time I took a half step *back*, raised my chin while nearly closing my right eye, and in a low but clear voice, I fired back, "Are you talkin' to me?"

Tony's face froze. Without giving him a chance I maintained control. "*I said,* 'Are you talkin' to me?' 'Cause if you are, you have to ask yourself a question. . . . Do you feel lucky?" I paused for effect. Around me, small gasps of admiration broke out from the group. Maintaining my stare, I lifted my chin up just a tad as I raised my voice, "Do you feel lucky? Well, do ya . . . *punk*?"

Tony's eyes seemed as if they would tear up. Maybe he felt bad for making my life hell. And now, I thought, he's learned his lesson. When Tony shook his head, that's when I knew I had him. Until he fired away with both fists to my face, shouting, "Lucky! I'm lucky 'cause I can kick your ass! Get it . . . *punk*?"

It was over before I hit the cement. Tony stormed off but

half his gang stayed behind. "Do it again!" one kid howled. Getting up, I wiped the blood from my lip, hoping my nose didn't burst with blood and I could find some tape for my glasses. Nodding in a way that conveyed the message "All right, show's over, geek boy got his butt kicked again," all I wanted to do was crawl under a rock. "Hey, it's okay," one of the boys said with sincerity. "We thought what you said was cool. How'd you do that? I mean, do it again, man!"

As much as I thought I was about to receive another pounding, I muttered the phrase again. "No," a different boy broke in, "do that, that thing, with your face and the eye." When the boy raised his voice, I flinched. "Dude, it's okay, it's cool, just go ahead and do it for us."

With the fear of being set up again racing through my veins, I reluctantly reared my head back, stared one of the boys down, and imitated Dirty Harry's voice. Seconds later the boys beamed at me. "Again!" they pleaded.

I repeated my performance almost a dozen times and threw in other imitations without thinking. I felt ten feet tall. Surprisingly the entire group, which had tormented me in the past whenever Tony was around, now gave me a combination of slaps on the palm of my hand. As the group departed, one of them warned me, "Pretty cool, but don't forget, you're still a doofus. And when Tony's around, I don't know you. You think I want him kickin' my ass? I don't think so. So, remember man, I don't know you."

Confused, all I could do was shake my head as if I agreed. As if sensing my bewilderment, a sharp-dressed kid came up to me. "Man, you don't get it, do ya?" I shook my head no. "Man, it's life in the food chain and this is the world. Just 'cause they be likin' you now don't mean squat. You dig?" I gave him a stupid grin. "Yo man, check it out. You ain't got it, can't find it, won't ever have it, even if a truck-load was dumped on ya. And your threads, I ain't even gonna go there. Then you be walking around like you's hunched over like, like that dude from Notra Dam. And in class, 'the teach' ask you a question, you be all spazzin' out. And man, I gots to tell ya, you look like a midget version of John Denver. The glasses, the hair, the whole getup; man, what's up with that? Rocky mountain high, my ass." He stopped for a moment, shaking his head. "You still don't dig it, do ya?"

I never heard anyone whip out so many words like that before. It was as if his mouth was dancing. I was mesmerized by the rhythm and timing of how the kid's words flowed so effortlessly. Before the cool boy left, he shook my hand in a way it had never been shaken. As he strutted off to the next class, he turned around, flashed me a sign, and shouted, "Peace!"

Back at home, in my room, I replayed everything the young man said to me. Before I entered kindergarten, I always knew I was different; that I didn't fit in. And since entering foster care, especially in junior high, I saw in the clearest sense how so many kids *acted*—either to fit in, impress, or just in a defensive manner. It seemed that if I stayed in the shadows, if I kept my mouth shut, and didn't fight back to try to defend myself, it didn't matter. Absolutely nothing worked for me.

As I had a short time ago, I knew I had two lives: my outside one, that everyone seemingly tormented and teased; then my inner one, the one that truly mattered, that only God and myself knew about. Deep down inside I knew I was smart. I was lightning fast in math, and whatever books interested me I'd absorb them into my mind. What the kids didn't know, what the tough kids could never understand, was the fact I had been put through a great deal and survived more than any of them could possibly fathom. From deep within I constantly told myself the same mantra I had since I was eight years old: *If I could survive all that I did alone, without any help, then what could I not possibly accomplish?*

Feeling myself become frustrated, I played the tape over in my mind for the millionth time that once I was eighteen and out of foster care, none of this would matter. Once I turned eighteen, I would be on my own, do as I pleased, and no one would ever bother me, ever again.

Yet in the core of my soul, all I ever wanted, all I ever craved was to belong. That someone my age would see that goodness within me. I wished I had a friend. A real friend. That night, as I prayed for my family that I was not allowed to see, I wished with all of my heart that I could simply fit in.

3

Wonderland

As a young teen, I came to believe that I was way too odd to ever belong or be accepted among kids my age. My reasoning came from a long internal list that basically broke down to a combination of my mannerisms, how I dressed, talked, my social awkwardness, and my almost nonexistent esteem. My only outlet was to withdraw to the one element that provided me a protective shield and a sense of worth: *work*. Deep down inside, without hesitation, I always knew I could complete whatever task was assigned. I only desired the chance to prove myself.

Part of my rationale lay within a growing paranoia I kept buried, that once I reached the legal age of eighteen, I would in effect "age out" of the foster care system. Within months of becoming a foster child, I learned from the terror in others' eyes who had approached that age how they feared becoming abandoned with nowhere or no one to turn to, mainly because they did what other kids did: date, go out with friends, and enjoy the wonders of their youth, rather than slave away and hoard every dollar for that inevitable day. Drawing from my compartmentalizing mind that I developed years before, I reasoned that, to my advantage, I could replace my lack of confidence and loneliness with getting ahead and by saving for my future all the sooner. Internally, years before foster care, my very existence, everything in my life was equated to sustenance. So as a young teen, the math was simple. When I became an adult, if I had no money, I had no food. No food, I starve. I starve, I die. And after all that I had been put through already, I could not allow that to happen.

With little pity or remorse for myself, while a majority of the cool kids from school bragged about what party they went to, how much they drank, who they kissed, how far they went, what bitchin' record they just bought, or seeing friends while hanging out at the mall, I quietly began my own enterprise. On the weekends I spent my time going from door to door asking to mow someone's grass or begging to perform any odd job around the neighborhood. Then, and even though I was scared to death, with my brand-new shoeshine kit in hand, I ventured into the seedy, darkened bars on the city's main street, promising the best shine for only fifty cents. As the months passed after a small growing spurt, I lied on my job application that I was a year older so I could work at the mall's restaurant as a busboy. With my long scrawny arms, I barely had the strength or endurance to carry the gray plastic tubs practically spilling over with dishes and glasses that were stacked like a pyramid. For months I lacked the skill and speed of snatching

34

the blistering-hot dishes and utensils that slid through the dishwasher as lightning fast as the other older boys, so hours after the mall had closed for the evening I completed my task while a frustrated assistant manager would sit on top of a cushioned swivel seat, while I frantically mopped the tiled floor under his feet.

As hard as it was, and as completely degraded as I felt and smelled at times, whenever I crossed the railroad tracks that led me to my foster home, inside I smiled. *I* earned a whopping $2.65 an hour. No one gave it to me and no one could take it from me. I earned it. Late into the night, as swirls of cold gray fog hugged the ground, with mounds of food and grease covering every inch of my face, matted hair, and shirt, I proudly walked home. While other kids were goofing off, I was little "big man" earning a living, paying taxes, putting in thirty to thirty-five hours a week. Then, during breaks, when school was out for more than a week, I easily worked more than sixty hours a week. My efforts counted where it mattered. I told myself *I was responsible*. In the working world, *I belonged*. It didn't matter if I stuttered, what clothes or shoes I wore, or what friends I had or didn't have. At work I was a real person. I belonged.

Even though I was only a freshman in high school, at work the tall, muscular boys and the pretty girls from the upper grades accepted me as their own. Yet just like in junior high, whenever I saw anyone I knew from work at school, I'd instantly duck my head and stride past so not to embarrass them or myself in public. Once, one of the girls I worked with at the fast-food restaurant, who was the most breathtaking girl in the entire school, yelled over from the other side of the hallway. In an instant I tensed up thinking I would get ridiculed. To my surprise, and in front of her bleach-blond, Farrah Fawcett–like feathered-hair friends, who chewed their mouthfuls of gum like cows chewing cud, she sashayed over, then winked at me before bending over and kissing me on the cheek. My knees buckled. As she withdrew, the ends of her hair brushed against my forehead. With my eyes closed I caught a whiff of her Charlie perfume. Hordes of kids froze in their tracks as they hooted and howled. As the blood raced to my cheeks, my world stopped. As a no-name, skinny, pimple-faced, invisible freshman, it was an extraordinary, one-of-a-kind moment. Then she turned on her wooden clogs and sashayed away, disappearing among the crowd.

That singular fleeting episode elevated my esteem for the longest time. For the most part, I was terrified of high school. To me, high school was the major leagues. Everything seemed so intensified—the lessons in class, the monumental amount of homework, the pressure of who belonged to what social cliques—while all the time I tried to glide by from class to class while hugging the shadows. After my "hallway kiss," I began to feel a little less fearful and intimidated, yet within days I moved again to a different home. I was crushed.

My newest foster parents, the Welshes, I thought were barely old enough to be parents themselves. In their mid-twenties and with three children of their own, the Welshes' carefree attitude was completely different from the other more mature, stricter homes. When I was told of another sudden move, I assumed I did something wrong—that my grades at school suffered from my work and therefore I had to be placed into yet another home. But to my surprise, the Welshes *and* I were moving from our dreary duplex into a home on the edge of the county. I hated the constant moves—adjusting to one home, getting lost as I found my way around a new city on my bike to find a job, or getting to know the layout of the new school and all that went with it. No wonder I never fit in, I told myself. As much as I became used to my high school, my main concern was where and how soon I could find another job.

Days later, in October of 1976, on a warm Saturday afternoon, I rode inside the back of the U-Haul trailer for just under an hour, with the sole intention of somehow protecting John Welsh's upright piano from rolling off in case the rope snapped. But it was only as John drove his ancient gold Chrysler on the bumpy freeway that I suddenly realized the only thing that kept John's prized household goods from spilling onto the freeway, in case the rattling U-Haul doors flew open, was my skinny frame and the death grip I had on a piece of frayed nylon that kept the jostling doors closed from within.

When John's car finally lurched to a stop, I flung open the doors before passing out from the car's exhaust fumes. After stepping outside, as my head cleared I wiped the grit from my eyes, then scanned my new surroundings. For a moment I couldn't believe it. Surely, I thought, Mr. Welsh had made a mistake. "We're gonna live *here*?" I shouted to no one in particular. As I strolled into the middle of the street, I heard John's confirmation. "Yep, this be the place." The entire neighborhood was something straight out of the 1960s television show *Leave It to Beaver*.

Everything was perfect. The homes seemed to glisten as if they were just painted. The front yards' grass were bright green and perfectly manicured. And every car seemed not only new, but shined as if just waxed. At one end of the street a tall, lanky boy shot basketball hoops, and at the other end of the block a small army of frenzied, well-dressed kids played in their front yard.

The only sounds besides the weeping willows' rustling leaves and the high-pitched children's laughter were muffled echoes of a hammer striking metal. I timidly stepped over to an open garage to sneak a better look. A man with taut muscles, black hair, and black-framed glasses was bent over and stopped when he must have sensed my presence. Too nervous to say anything, I shrugged my shoulders and simply stared. After a few seconds, the man straightened his posture, seemingly wondering what I wanted. With my mouth beginning to dry, I blurted, "So . . . whatcha doin'?"

Wiping the sweat from his creased forehead, the man replied, "Working."

Fascinated by the man's vintage orange Chevy truck parked in the driveway, I lingered. "I just, just moved in," I stumbled, while pointing at the U-Haul trailer. "We're gonna be neighbors," I stupidly added, as if he hadn't already figured this out.

The man replied with a thin smile. He waved his hammer as if to move me along, and he emphasized, "I'm busy, and you should be helping your father."

Speaking faster than I could think, I corrected, "Oh . . . he's not my dad. We're not relat—"

After raising an eyebrow at me, the mechanic gave me a quick glance up and down. Then without a word, he again waved his hammer, telling me to move on before returning to his task.

For most of my childhood, and the last two years while in foster care, I had seen *that* look a million times before. Strolling across the street, I told myself not only what a spaz I was, but what a jerk the man in the garage was. I found out some time later that I had just met Dan Brazell.

Later that night as I lay on the top bunk with my hands clasped behind my head and the window cracked open, I listened to the wind run through the weeping willows. With a slight inhale, I absorbed the fragrance from the nearby jasmine. There were no sounds of police or fire sirens racing up and down Main Street. I didn't live in a run-down neighborhood, with broken rusted-out cars resting on cinder blocks. I didn't have to endure another night of listening to some couple yelling from the other side of the duplex, or pulsating music that reverberated from three houses away. As I closed my eyes, I felt a quiet sense of calmness.

The next Monday, in the afternoon, my mundane life took a drastic turn when two boys about my age, who had watched me unload the Welshes' belongings the entire weekend, strolled over to introduce themselves. Having glanced at them both on and off during the last two days, I didn't feel threatened or intimidated in any way. The taller of the two, Dave Howard, had wide eyes that seemed to drip with enthusiasm, with a matching grin as if craving for something to happen. Paul Brazell, slightly shorter than me, had intense eyes, as if he were constantly contemplating several things at once.

With an inquisitive gaze Paul jumped in with a query, "My dad says those folks aren't your parents. So . . . what's the deal?"

I immediately knew where this was heading. Once they confirmed what I felt they already knew, Paul would then distract me with a few choice sentences, while David would move in for the kill.

"I'm, uh . . . a . . . foster kid," I mumbled.

Rearing his head back, David roared, "A foster kid? . . . " Stepping back, I plotted where to flee before Howard might raise his fist. Looking down at me, David gave me a leering smirk. As if pausing for effect, he finally blurted, "Cool, man. So, what's it like not to have to live with your parents? You must get away with a lot, eh?"

I breathed a sigh of relief that I wasn't about to be ridiculed, but before I had a chance to smile, Paul huffed, "I wouldn't mind not living with mine."

Eager to get to know them, I asked, "So, what's it like to live here?"

Both Paul and David didn't seem to share my excitement. While Paul continued to study me, David shrugged his shoulders. "It's no big deal."

Stunned in disbelief, I fired back, "No way! I mean, look at this place—the trees, the homes—it's so *Stepford*. I've never, and I mean never, seen *anything* like this before." I knew I was becoming overly emotional about something that seemed so mundane, but I persisted. "So . . . what's it like to live *here*?"

For a few moments the three of us shuffled our feet in silence. With a slight twinkle in his eye, David Howard smiled at me. David and I seemed to feel the same sense of appreciation. After a few moments of awkward silence Paul turned to point toward his front yard, explaining how his father, Dan, through his own sweat and ingenuity over the years, had turned it into the pride of the neighborhood; including resurfacing the grass, the brick walkway, and brick fencing. The more the three of us carried on the conversation, the more I realized I was part of something. I wasn't the outsider who never fit in, who got tormented or beat up simply because I was different. As the sun's rays seemed to fade, from deep inside, for the life of me, I couldn't stop smiling. In a seemingly ordinary everyday moment, I raised my hand to shield my face, but it wasn't from fear or an act of defense, but to help keep my eyes from squinting from the setting sun. I didn't want to lose a second of being with David and Paul.

"So," Paul inquired, "at the other places you lived at, what did you do . . . for fun? What'd ya do?"

I shrugged before answering, "Well, after coming home

from high school I'd go to work. On the weekends I put in a full-time shift, then maybe once in a while I'd go to the movies."

David's eyes grew wide. "You work full time?"

I nodded my head. "Yeah, it's no big deal. I've been doing it for a . . ."

"Man," Howard grinned. "You must be rich. What ya gonna do, buy a car? That would be bitchin'."

"Nope." I brushed it off. "I, uh, just save money; you know, unless I buy clothes or something." As I answered I realized I had never given much thought to buying a car. For years my mind-set had been driven by pure survival.

"You get to buy your own clothes?" Howard asked.

"My mom still takes me shopping. It's such a drag. I hate it when she checks the waist by pulling up on the pants in front of everybody." Paul rolled his eyes.

"That's 'cause you're so cute," Howard teased. "So, Pelz, do you have a driver's license or a permit? 'Cause if you had a car, we could cruise El Camino Real, pick up chicks, and get lucky," David drooled.

"No!" Paul shouted. "He doesn't have a license; if he did, he wouldn't be talking to us. Duh!" Turning toward me, Paul stated, "You have to forgive Howie; he's been dropped on the head one too many times."

Contorting his face, David imitated, "That's right, George. Dropped on the head, I was, 'cause I likes to tend da rabbits. Gonna tend da rabbits. That's what I'm gonna do, get a place of my own and tend da rabbits."

"Man!" I exclaimed, "That's my all-time favorite book!"

"A book?" Howard asked. "I got it from a cartoon."

"Yo, Deputy Dawg," Paul interrupted, "it's a book. *Of Mice and Men.* You know, a couple of guys working all over, trying to scrape up enough so they can have a place of their own."

Acting as if he didn't understand, Howard remained still. "Yeah," I agreed. "These two guys who don't fit in, they work at this camp with other men who band together to share their dream, so they can live and no one can bother them. You see, all they wanted was to have their own home. A band of brothers in their own home. . . ." My voice trailed off.

Howard again smiled. I shook my head, discovering that he knew all along about the story he had probably read in junior high, like I had a few years ago. "We could be a band of brothers."

"I'd be Lenny," Paul announced.

Imitating the voice I did in drama class, I said, "An, an I be, be George."

"What about me?" David whined. "What's my character?"

"You'd be the rabbit," Paul stated while smiling at me for encouragement.

"Definitely," I seconded. "You'd be the rabbit."

Giving Howard a deviant look, Paul rationalized, "In case you pissed us off, I could whack you on the head, and cook you for stew."

The three of us bantered back and forth, teasing one another about who'd be who in our little game. We rambled back and forth across the street until Paul's mother shouted it was time for dinner. After teasing Paul as he left that he would be the ill-fated *rabbit*, David and I stood facing the sun's last rays until he, too, was called home for dinner. Feeling vulnerable and suddenly alone as David raced down the block toward home, I shouted, "See, ya! See ya tomorrow!"

Howard stopped, ran back, and patted my shoulder. "Lenny eat fast for George, so we can tend da rabbits." Then dropping the act, David leaned close to say, "I'll be back in a few. I'll see ya right after dinner. Then we'll have some fun. Trust me, *you are so gonna love living here.*"

4

The Neighborhood Threat

Within days of moving into Duinsmoore Way, the once serene neighborhood transformed into a playground of reckless abandon. As a pencil-thin, four-eyed, pimple-infested, shaggy-haired teen with no esteem, I had become the epitome of terror. And it all started with the minibikes.

When John Welsh drove up with the final load of belongings containing my rusted minibike, Paul and David rushed over to ogle at my prize. After years of hoarding every dollar I could—that wasn't spent on bell-bottom jeans or a psychedelic rayon shirt, or whenever I'd splurge on a movie or ABBA's latest record—one day on a whim I had purchased a motorized minibike for the paltry sum of $35.00. As Paul and David stood gawking at the bike, they acted like they'd never seen one before. To me it wasn't all that much to look at. The threads on both tires were practically bare, the single horsepower Briggs & Stratton lawn mower engine was louder than a jet engine, and it accelerated as fast as a turtle crawling uphill against the wind. My vehicle had no brakes and slowed only when I mashed the heels of my worn Adidas tennis shoes to the pavement. On the plus side, the faded red, tubular frame acted as a sponge to either absorb or hide the rust, the grayish-black exhaust, and the dark sticky oil that oozed from every seal of every gasket.

And yet the bike was my baby. "Pretty cool, ay?" I pointed as Paul knelt down for a closer look. His eyes inspecting every part, Paul simply nodded. After a few moments Paul stepped away allowing David, who was smiling from ear to ear, his turn to examine the bike.

"So, how fast does it go?" David asked.

With my hands folded against my chest I smiled. "Thirty . . . maybe forty miles per hour," I smugly lied.

"No way, dude!" Howard shot back.

"Oh yeah," I justified, "this baby rips." *This was way too easy,* I thought to myself. I knew I had David totally suckered until I heard the distinctive rumbling echo from behind me. Spinning around, my cool facade instantly dissolved when I discovered Paul sitting triumphantly on a gleaming metallic-sliver and blue-green minibike.

From behind, David punched me in the shoulder as he leaned over and stated, "Pretty cool, ay?"

After Paul informed me how his father had built the bike for him as a Christmas present, all I could do was marvel while he rattled off in meticulous detail the bike's features, ranging from the rear drum brake system, the smooth-idling, two-and-a-half horsepower motor, down to the slick black grip handles.

David couldn't resist. "Hey, Paul. Pelz says his bike can

go thirty, even forty miles per hour. You two oughta race!"
Howard's words were the neighborhood's undoing. Within
minutes Paul and I were revving our minibikes up and
down the street. Then again, and again and again, until
both of us ran out of gas. By an embarrassing margin, Paul
always won. In the days to follow, the races continued with
the same results: Paul with his superior machine would
always spring ahead, while I pumped my feet like Fred
Flintstone propelling his prehistoric car. The most my dilapidated minibike could do was cough before belching a
cloud of dark smoke, *then* begin putting its way after Paul,
who, by that time, was so far ahead it was degrading to
even try.

In the weeks to follow I became obsessed, but surprisingly it was not with my usual self-induced paranoid state
of finding more jobs—so that I could exhaust every inch of
myself day after day, stashing away a few bucks from a
measly paycheck so I wouldn't starve in the future. This
constant pressure was becoming too much. As proud as I
was of being a young teen working in an adult world, I
didn't know how long I could keep up the frantic, almost
suicidal pace. And yet, it was all so *normal* for *me:* Get up,
go to school, do homework between classes, at lunch, in the
bathroom stall, wherever. Blitz home, change clothes, run
off to work. Tuesdays, Thursdays, and every other Friday
and Saturday I'd be a busboy at the Sizzler restaurant, but
on Mondays and Wednesdays I'd work at the fast-food
joint on the other side of town, while other days I'd fill in at
the plastics factory during the swing shift and would shine

shoes in between. Pedal the bike, lean into the wind, can't be late. Work hard, work fast, don't stop, don't quit, don't think, just do. Go, go, go, go!

And at least when I worked, I felt less guilty, less dirty about my former life or the fact that my brothers were still under the rule of my disturbed mother. My sweat, my labor, was penitence for me. But every afternoon I spent with David and Paul goofing off, babbling away about nothing for hours, meant $10 a day less for me to hoard. Part of me could not believe that I would even contemplate the *idea* of *not* constantly pushing myself to extremes on a daily basis. But yearning to be with my friends was a sensation so strong that it was beyond anything else I had ever experienced.

With the garage door wide open and the evening breeze seeping in as I tinkered with my minibike, I willingly brushed aside my guilt. I began to focus my attention on my *new* obsession: beating Paul. Even after I rinsed out my lime-green spongelike air filter, tightened my loose chain that rattled from the rear wheel's sprocket, adjusted the carburetor idle to full open, then gave the bike a bath in gasoline to remove the crud and baked-on oil splotches, as if to somehow make my motorized relic more aerodynamic, I knew my chances were still nil. The math was obvious: Paul had an engine that didn't constantly sputter, had more horsepower, and brakes that allowed him to go faster for longer distances . . . and he weighed far less than me.

My only chance was to somehow outthink my opponent. If in the past I could concoct painstaking plans to the slightest movement that helped me survive in my abnormal environment, or to outwit the pack of bullies from junior high and high school, I could certainly apply that same technique to outsmart Paul.

The next afternoon, after briefing David on my plan, he suggested to Paul that instead of racing the length of the block, we'd make the circuit around the entire neighborhood. I figured I needed the extra time and distance for everything to come together. *Yes,* I informed myself, *Paul and his bike were superior, but his one folly, his only mistake was he had become complacent.* After eating his fumes and following Paul dozens of times, I had gotten to know his riding style. *This* was my strategy: While Paul always rode in the middle of the street, I would now shave every corner. When Paul would apply his brake before taking a corner, my plan was to jam my bike's throttle wide open. For all his adjustments, for all his computations, Paul never rode full out. And now I would. Nothing would stop me. As excited as I was from a swirling sense of fear, I knew I could do it. For years I had kept my confidence locked away deep inside to survive my mother. But now I could apply it to something adventurous.

With David as the demented starter for the great race, Paul and I revved our engines as if we were Indy-500 Formula-1 race car drivers. In front and behind Paul and me, it was hard not to notice how both sides of the block had become lined with clusters of small kids, who protected themselves behind parked cars that scattered the driveways. While their eyes opened wide in anticipation, some of the kids' mouths hung as if they were salivating for some up close eye-candy carnage. Milking his immortal place in the annals of Duinsmoore Way, Howard bellowed, "Gentlemen . . . start your engines!" It didn't seem to matter that no one could hear David due to the deafening roar of the bikes, making more noise and pollution than the supersonic Concorde jet aircraft. Quick to recover, and as if trying to redeem his error, David raised a finger before again bellowing to half the audience who cowered behind the cars' bumpers, "I want a clean race. No hitting below the belt. No spitting. And no, uh, banana peels in the street. On my mark, on the count of three. One, two, two and a half, two and three quarters . . ."

Paul was smart enough to get the jump. Before I knew it, he was blazing away at full steam, while I leaned forward, frantically peddling to obtain single-digit speed. As my minibike gained momentum, Paul, as usual, rode in the middle of the street without a care in the world. Before taking the first corner, Paul let up on the gas and turned to check on my position, before gently applying his brake.

That's when I made my move. A few seconds later, approaching the same corner, I scooted my butt off my moldy seat and leaned my body and minibike over in a sudden ninety-degree turn, as if I were the legendary motorcycle racer Kenny Roberts. To my surprise, besides a few sparks from the frame's peg, I executed the maneuver without killing myself. I was too stupid to be scared. And Paul was too bewildered to believe that I was now nearly beside him, until he again leaned forward and gunned his throttle.

Staying on the inside of the street I gained a few seconds before I readied myself for the next corner, rolled out, sucked in another deep breath, and honed in on the final turn. Beginning to feel a little cocky, and with Paul just ahead, I again performed my "Kenny Roberts" tactic, when I felt the minibike's left peg dig into the pavement. Stealing a quick glance, I saw a shower of orange sparks fly by my sneaker.

Being preoccupied with the possibility of my shoe catching fire was my mistake. A second after straightening the minibike upright, I stared into the eyes of a small girl who stood frozen directly in front of me, screaming at the top of her lungs. Time seemed to stand still as I could see with perfect clarity the girl's pretty floral dress and the bright yellow ribbon in her ponytail. The child's high-pitched wail brought me out of my time warp. Even as I let off the gas and began to drag my heels, I knew it wasn't enough. At the same time and to the far left, another girl, the older sister, I assumed, sprang up and ran to pluck her screaming sister from impending doom. Yet to the right of me, just a few feet away, Paul seemed oblivious. I thought for sure Paul, realizing the situation and knowing I had no brakes, would slow down so I could zip in front of him to avoid colliding with him and, more important, avoid the terrified child. To make matters worse, to the left and just behind the girl was a jumbo-sized station wagon resting near the sidewalk that I had somehow not seen before we started the race.

My arms seemed paralyzed as I couldn't help but *steer*

my bike directly *at* the girl. My brain screamed, *Oh my God, I'm gonna hit her! I'm gonna hit her!* like a broken record. My head began to replay the countless times how I could never do anything right—how incredibly stupid I always was, how much hardship I had constantly caused, or how I always, always screwed up everything. I never had the guts to change the outcome, to alter my course. I knew I would forever be destined to fail. I hated myself for not doing something, anything to avoid another Pelzer-induced disaster.

All I could do was tell myself to close my eyes, suck in a deep breath, tense my feeble body, and pray the girl would miraculously evaporate.

As I began to inhale, my mind spun into overdrive. My head suddenly began playing James Bond theme music. I tensed my face and analyzed my predicament. In front, the girl remained statuesque and had more air in her lungs than an opera singer, as she proceeded to wail. My mind began spinning off various options. Jumping off the bike wouldn't work—either me or the minibike might somehow become entangled with the child. To the right, Paul was still absorbed in the race and continued on his heading. If I deliberately collided with him, there was still a chance I'd hit the girl. The only option was to lean to the left, then lay the bike down and into the front of the Spruce Goose–sized station wagon. With any luck I would roll under the car. My only concerns were that the bike would slide under with me, trapping me under the car, or that I would somehow flip up and crash against the windshield. Either way, I was about to ruin one of my favorite pair of expensive bell-bottom jeans.

As I positioned myself for the maneuver by sliding my butt off the seat, I suddenly saw an opportunity. Between the girl and the front bumper of the car was a few feet of clearance. By staring directly at the child and the car, I had only had a one-dimensional view. I had somehow stupidly become locked into the idea that they were both side by side. But there was only a small gap and worth the chance. Tensing my face, I committed by opening the throttle wide open, tilted the bike as far left as it would go, while praying the peg didn't dig in and flip me and the bike over. As I passed the girl, her eyes followed me as she sucked in another breath to scream. I wanted to turn my head and nod to her that everything was going to be fine, but I was too focused on not screwing up. Suddenly the child jerked her head toward me. I could imagine her jumping out in front of the minibike. I glanced at her feet, which were still planted and facing the middle of the street. I knew if she did move, by the time her feet went into motion I would be behind her while she would be running forward, away from me. A fraction of a second after breezing past the girl, I swung the bike over to the right, missing the shiny chromed bumper by a few feet.

Minutes after the near catastrophe, I sat near my bike, which lay on its side, while fighting to catch my breath. I wanted to run up the street to check on the girl, but the intimidating glares from a group of adults surrounding the crying child kept me away. Howard was the first one to break the silence. "Man, that was *too cool*. I thought for sure you were gonna get creamed. I just wish I had my mom's camera."

Catching my breath, I leaned back and, oddly enough, soaked in the praise. For once in my life I didn't flinch, I didn't choke. *I actually did something right.* Just a couple of years before when I had tried out for football in junior high, I was the smallest, scrawniest kid on the team. I couldn't run, catch, block a mannequin, or even snap the football. I always felt an overwhelming pressure swell up inside me, to the point that I'd hike the football up and over the quarterback's head. Even as a preschooler, whenever my mother would stand over me, my fingers trembled so bad that I couldn't tie my shoes. I never did well under any kind of pressure, especially if someone was in the vicinity. But just a few minutes ago I succeeded. With all that was swirling around me, I had a clear vision. I found a sense of calmness and followed through. I had threaded the eye of the needle.

And yet part of me wanted nothing more than to rip into Paul. *"Why didn't you back off or give me some room?!"*

Probably sensing my anger, Paul sat on his prize with his arms crossed and looked up and replied, "Oh, it wasn't as close as you think. You were gonna miss her by at least a mile."

I clamped my mouth shut, but inside my head I let loose, *That's not the point! You . . . you . . . butt head! I got no brakes to slow down, no room to maneuver, the girl could've bolted like a scared horse, and I could have become a hood ornament!*

THE PRIVILEGE OF YOUTH

A few seconds later my anger subsided, and Paul's stoic pose loosened. "You should have seen your face, man. If I were you, I'd check my shorts," Paul laughed.

I had suddenly become infamous. The incident about "that foster kid who tried to run down little Amy" became the ongoing topic of the tranquil block. No adult ever approached me, but Paul and David kept me well informed: I was marked. Whenever I'd cross the street to Paul's house or stroll down to David's, nearly everyone would suddenly snap their heads in another direction to avoid looking at me.

The next Sunday afternoon, the three of us lay on our backs on an old shed in the Welshes' backyard. This became our hangout. At times we would just lie still, not uttering a word, staring straight up at the birds fluttering above us in the trees. The weekend before, Paul had convinced me that if I walked from one edge of the shed to the other and maintained the same pace, my momentum would allow my feet to catch onto the large overlapping branch of a nearby tree. With absolute calmness Paul assured me that he had figured it all out. "Besides," Paul had shrugged, "you're only a few feet off the ground. And, uh, if you fall, you'd just have to grab on to a branch, to break your fall."

"Dude," David added, "it's cool. You gotta do it!"

Taking a deep breath while keeping my chin up, I was way too scared to back down from a "dare." I took large military-like steps, and with the precision of a drill cadet I marched perfectly straight off the shed. When my right foot stepped into space, I snapped my head down—discovering Paul's meticulous calculations were absolute nonsense—as the nearest branch was just beyond reach. My forward momentum lasted a nanosecond before Newton's law of physics went into effect. Before my mind could engage my mouth to cry out for help, my arms shot straight up, grabbing only molecules. My body then pitched forward, hitting every branch until I flipped over, landing squarely on my back with a sickening thud.

Above me, Paul and David seemed to be in the far end of a long dark tunnel, giggling back down at me. My lips went dry. I couldn't lift my arms or move my fingers to gesture to them to help me. As my vision sharpened, a jarring pain crept up my back. For an instant I thought I'd live out my life in a wheelchair for something so incredibly stupid. But as my head cleared and my limbs responded, I knew I was going to be fine enough to choke the life out of both Paul and David.

Seven days after nearly becoming paralyzed, the three of us sat with our feet dangling over the edge of the shed. Breaking the silence, for no apparent reason Paul let out a laugh. "I still can't believe you did that last week, Pelzer," he said, shaking his head.

David snickered, "You should have heard it. It was like . . . someone dropping a bag of wet flour," he emphasized with a closed fist hitting the palm of his other hand.

"No," Paul corrected, "more like a sack of cement. And if you look, you can still see your outline. I mean it, stand up and check it out. Really, if you *lean over*, you can just make out where you fell. Come on, check it out."

"After you," I offered with a wave of my hand.

Looking at one another the three of us broke out in laughter. "What a week." David huffed. Glancing at him for a moment, I knew where the conversation was heading. Even though we had all rehashed "the Amy incident" dozens of times, whenever any of us began the tale it was as if it had just happened.

"What were you thinking, when you came barreling down the street and came face-to-face with Amy?" David grilled. "I mean, weren't you scared?"

I, too, had reveled about the incident, but in the late afternoon sun, while the world seemed still, I searched for the moral perspective. "Yeah, I guess . . . I mean, I don't . . . I dunno," I stammered. "When I first saw Amy, yeah I was afraid. Part of me locked up and thought for sure I was gonna slam into her. And then, part of me washed it away and figured as long as Amy stayed still, by the time she did anything I would have already passed her. I just didn't want to wipe out and hit her or the car. I took a chance. I got lucky. That's all it was, luck," I nodded to David and Paul as well as to myself.

"But Pelz," David followed up, "man, you were like . . . like so intense. It's like you were fearless or something. I gotta tell ya, man, ever since I met you, I can't figure you out. It's like everything for you is the first time. Riding bikes, hanging out, or even this shed, man, you really dig this shed."

I knew what David was getting at and, by Paul's expression, he felt the same. "Remember as kids, when our parents would take us on summer vacation?" I asked.

"Yeah," Paul interrupted, "grandmas! *'Oh, look how much he's grown! Here's a nickel, why don't you run down and go buy you a nice piece of taffy.'* All they do is smell like formaldehyde and always want to bend down and squeeze your cheeks. One time, by accident, I looked down my grandma's blouse. Man, that was gross."

"Oh, you loved it!" David fired back. "Go on, Pelz."

"Anyway, at that time it was just my two brothers and me, and my mom and dad would take us to the Russian River. Man, the trees were kinda like this but only redwoods, and they were huge, as tall as skyscrapers. Ron, Stan, and I would play outside all day on this tree stump or just goof around doin' nothin'. It was so cool. Back then I felt safe. No matter what happened, no matter what I did, everything was gonna be cool. Everything would turn out okay. That's why I like hanging out here. It's so peaceful. You get away from all the everyday bullshit."

"I know what you mean," Paul huffed.

"What are you griping about?" David jumped in.

"You know, my dad's always on my case, and my mom's always telling me what to do. I'm not even supposed to be here. If she finds out, I can get into trouble. It's like I can't do anything."

David shook his head. "You're an altar boy; you're not

supposed to be doing anything. What's the diff', same at my place. Besides, your dad's, like, way cool."

Deflecting, Paul turned to me. "I bet it's easier at your place."

"Definitely. It's weird though; it's like they don't care," I replied while realizing that out of all the foster parents I had had, John and Linda were extremely easygoing.

"So, what's it like?" David asked. "I mean, what do you do?"

"I dunno, same as anyone else. Help out with chores, do as they say . . . you know, normal stuff," I answered.

"But being a foster kid, that's gotta be weird," Howard stated.

Looking up at the trees and without thinking I blurted, "I gotta say something. I uh, I've seen some stuff. . . . For years, every day, *and I mean every day,* I was terrified of my own shadow. I was so scared of every move I made. I couldn't even pee straight. You're taking a leak and your hand's shaking and you get piss all over your pants and shoes. Do you have any idea what that's like? When I was put into foster care, I somehow thought everything would change," I emphasized, snapping my fingers. "But at school, man, I got my ass kicked, stomped, beaten, you name it, every day. New kid this, skinny rat that, hey four eyes. I've heard it all. Man, what a pain. And all I wanted was to be like everyone else; you know, fit in. I never really had friends. In the beginning Ron, Stan, and I were close before things turned bad. My family, my brothers, man, they all hate me.

59

"When you're in the system, in foster care, you can't get too close 'cause you move around so much. You don't know who to trust. You never fit in. You keep your wall up, so you don't get hurt. The only time I used to fit in was when I worked. I'd channel everything into that. But the thing is with *you guys*, I ain't scared. I mean it, I'm *not* scared. I don't have to prove myself; you guys accept me. It's like . . . like I belong. With you two it's like I'm this totally different guy, who's not afraid and can do anything. You know what I mean?"

"Yeah, man," David replied. "Totally, I get it."

"I dunno," Paul warned, "you're pretty intense. You didn't see that look on your face."

"Well, next time, move the hell outta the way," I berated.

"Never!" Paul fired back.

The remainder of the afternoon the three of us rehashed the Amy incident over and over again until it included sound effects and Paul's desire to have somehow filmed the event, as if he were the director of the movie *Jaws*. As the sun's rays slid past the trees, I took in a deep breath. I turned to Paul and David and merely stated, "Today was a good day."

Savoring the moment, with our hands behind our heads, the three of us gazed upward and nodded in unison.

"So," David chimed in, "what are we gonna do *tomorrow*?"

5

Brotherhood

With "the Amy incident" still fresh in our minds—and especially on the minds of those in the neighborhood—late one afternoon the three of us decided to implement what Paul designated as the "ROEs": the Rules of Engagement. Once initiated, "the rules" would somehow prevent us from diving too far into the depths of despair. We rarely had the vaguest idea of what we might do, for we only craved to do *something* and *now*. After an hour of mindless chatter in the heart of Mr. Brazell's garage, Paul pulled in the reins. "Look, man. This is serious. You two quit goofin' around. Grow up, will ya. We gotta come up with a plan."

By the edge in Paul's voice, David and I suddenly dropped our "Three Stooges" act. Whatever commotion we caused, David Howard and I knew it was Paul who took the most heat for our escapades. Because of the notoriety of Paul's family, either through the neighborhood, church, or good deeds offered by Mr. Brazell, the moment anyone saw anything, within the speed of light and as if through telepathic means, it was beamed over to Paul's mother, Beth. Even when Paul, David, and I were in the process of one of our stunts, Mrs. Brazell somehow knew everything and Paul was instantly busted. Sometimes we became so terrified of Mrs. Brazell that the three of us would huddle close together, scheming in whispered tones behind my backyard shed, to form a protective barrier to Beth's penetrating radar.

While David Howard was rarely reprimanded by his parents, I was basically left alone. Finally, being in foster care had its advantages. Because John and Linda slaved away at dead-end jobs they both despised, by the end of the day when they'd drag themselves home, John and Linda still had to contend with their three small children. By helping out with the housework I could then make myself scarce, and I somehow became immune to any firm sense of discipline.

Of the three of us, I was like a hyperactive puppy— constantly in motion, looking to get my wet nose into everything all at once. After Paul again snapped at me, I calmed down enough for the three of us to define our new guidelines. As the afternoon faded into dinnertime, Paul, David, and I came up with a quasi set of ROEs, which to us made perfect sense: Rule Number One: *No Girls*. While alluring and mysterious as they were, none of us had a "pick-up mobile," money, cool clothes, social skills, or looks. We also figured that girls would sooner or later not only land us in trouble, but more important they would take away from our time together. The fact that no girl with any sense would have anything to do with us, mattered very little. Of course, in front of one another, we acted as if girls were no big deal. Yet alone with Paul, or especially with David, we'd all drool whenever one of the older, mature girls from the end of the street would sashay by in a short green plaid skirt. My accomplice and I would hide out, covering our giggling mouths in the hopes that a sudden gust of wind would blow by—just like it did to Marilyn Monroe.

The second parameter: *No Guns.* No real weapons of any kind at any time. Although the Duinsmoore neighborhood and nearby mansions seemed like something out of Beverly Hills, across the freeway it was like a Middle East war zone with stories of rampant gangs, shootings, and occasional drive-bys. Simply put, this rule was made to avoid serious trouble. But when David brought up the fact that I had a pellet gun, Paul's recent acquisition of a BB gun, and David's tiny BB gun rifle that he had had for years, we convinced ourselves that *technically* our arsenal was merely "toy guns" and that we could continue to use them for the sole purpose of target practice.

As deliberately silly and tame as the first two "Rules of Engagement" were, the third rule—the final declaration—Paul, David, and I took as absolute gospel. It was unbreakable: *No Drugs.* No using, dealing, or associating with anyone who did. Period. During our time together we all commented on what we saw firsthand in parts of the city, schools, or with those we knew and how narcotics took its toll. As immature as we acted, as reckless as we appeared to be in front of others, there was no doubt for any of us on the seriousness of this core belief.

"It will mess you up," Paul stated.

"I can't live that way," I said, shaking my head.

"That's some sick shit and it will kill ya, plain and simple, man," David said, looking straight into our eyes.

"So," Paul warned, "this is it. The ROEs. Once we agree, there's no turning back. Any questions?"

In an instant David and I shot each other a wide grin. Both of us could have acted like Moe and Curly of "The Three Stooges" and taken the debate in a zillion different directions, but for once David and I remained quiet and smiled.

"You know this means we're brothers," David said as he shook his head.

"This is the real deal," Paul reassured. "We look out for one another. Friends, forever."

I couldn't believe my ears. Part of me wanted to cry. "One for all and all for one!"

Paul, David, and I stacked our hands one on top of the other. "Deal," one said.

"Deal," the other agreed.

"Deal," I quickly echoed before taking a moment to turn to them and pledge, "Brothers!"

"Now we should prick our fingers, draw blood, and shake hands!" David blurted.

"No way, this ain't no Tom Sawyer novel. Besides, I don't know where your finger's been," Paul teased as David crinkled his face and lifted his finger to his nose.

The Privilege of Youth

We stood staring at one another as the moment slipped away, until Paul's eyes lit up. "Here!" Paul shouted as he leaned over to his father's workbench and grabbed an open-end wrench. "No girls, no guns, and no drugs. We take care of each other for now and forever. If one falls, the others will pick 'em up." With his fingers spread on top of the shiny wrench laying on the workbench, Paul smiled. *"Brothers."*

"Brothers," David thundered, with his fingers wrapped around Paul's.

"Brothers," I shouted.

I had been aching for so long to belong, to truly be part of something, and for once to not be on the outside looking in. With the word *brothers* echoing in my ears, my mind began to relive parts of my former life. As a small child at home, my oldest brother, Ron, always seemed to keep close watch over me, while Stan, my youngest brother at the time, was my best friend at elementary school, until I was singled out by my volatile, alcoholic mother who then decreed that my brothers were not allowed to have anything to do with me, that for some reason, I was the cause for whatever problems existed within the family. Over a short time I had become de facto, not a member of the family, to the point that I had become invisible to Ron, Stan, and even my drunken father. My mother had forbidden any of them to even utter my name.

So, with a few exchanged words and a set of flesh and bone stacked on top of one another, a bond became forged.

Like a preschooler on Christmas morning, I stood in wide-eyed wonderment, not only at Paul and David but the setting of our oath. Now loitering just inside the door of Mr. Brazell's garage, the three of us huddled by Paul's father's newly built customized tool bench that held every wrench, group of hammers, pliers, and an endless array of screwdrivers that were perfectly outlined with a black marker against the wall under a set of handcrafted cabinets. Behind every cabinet door were supplies for every occasion: various sandpaper, stacked in accordance to its grade; glues like Bondo to fill in and smooth out metal dents; and every conceivable file known to man. Attached below the cabinets was a collection of small jars that held an assortment of screws, tacks, nuts, bolts, washers, and anything else that Mr. Brazell thought necessary. I stared in amazement at what must have been the extensive planning, patience, and the deliberate function of every item of Mr. Brazell's private world, and it seemed to radiate a sense of calmness.

Before my tingling fingers could explore, Paul warned me off with a wave of his hand, while plucking with his other hand an open-end wrench. Even though for weeks I had constantly praised his father's garage, Paul seemed to only shrug his shoulders as if it were no big deal. While I would always nod my head slightly, brushing off yet another miscommunication on my behalf, in my heart I knew Mr. Brazell's garage had an extraordinary and haunting significance for me.

* * *

THE PRIVILEGE OF YOUTH

Before entering foster care, as a form of humiliation—when not performing an endless list of chores for my mother—during my "off time" I was commanded to either sit on top of my hands or stand ramrod straight at the base of a set of wooden stairs in a dark basement/garage. To further cheapen my existence, many times the garage became my bedroom, and my bed an army surplus World War II green cot that I'd unfold at night. I quickly learned to set up the canvas cot by the front bumper of the family station wagon and the furnace to capture any possible heat. When I sat or stood at the bottom of the stairs, I'd always strain my eyes left to capture the outline of my father's narrow, endless workbench, which held a scattered array of hand and power tools. A combative marriage would eventually drive him away, leaving his once-proud domain to become invaded by abandoned spider webs and heaps of grayish-black dust. My only fond memory of the bench and its heyday was a solitary moment out of the blue, when as a preschooler clinging to my father's side, he unexpectedly plucked me up and plopped me down on top of his sacred territory with a firm warning of not to touch a thing. Sure to obey, I tilted my head up, staring at a giant of a man, with shiny ribbed-combed black hair, who could perform any feats of wonder and did so with the aid of magical-like devices from his workbench. At the time, Father was my very own Superman and the workbench area was his fortress of solitude. To be in the fortress with my superhero was beyond any expression a mere child could offer.

* * *

Now, years later, with a new lease on life, for me to be standing within the fringes of Mr. Brazell's workplace, where clear bright light shined in every crevice, where hundreds upon hundreds of instruments seemed to glisten like polished silver, made my former life seem like some sketchy, one-time kindergarten-like nightmare. I now beamed with a quiet sense of pride that I didn't have before. Upon entering foster care, I was so perfectly ignorant; at my first foster home I could not distinguish the difference between a nut, a bolt, the function of a washer, let alone the difference between a flat head and a Phillips screwdriver. Since then I acquired a simple set of no-name token tools that I used to maintain my bicycle and minibike, and since moving to Duinsmoore and studying Mr. Brazell, I took great pride to always wipe off my instruments with a soft rag that had a dab of gasoline to remove any grime. Before carefully storing them in my battered red tin carrying case, I'd lift up my tools against the flickering lightbulb in Mr. Welsh's garage, inspecting for any scratch, smudge, or oil that somehow might belittle them.

Whenever I would have to wait on Paul, I'd stand on the driveway just beyond Mr. Brazell's view, admiring his deliberate moves, then search for that single moment—that satisfying look on his tired face whenever Paul's father completed a task as he wiped the sweat off his wrinkled forehead before strolling over to the back of the garage to wash his hands. After a few weeks of spying, one afternoon, without thinking, while Mr. Brazell was in the back scrubbing his hands, I snatched a broom and began meticulously sweeping the floor. I wanted to, I *had* to, show Mr. Brazell that *I* was the best floor sweeper of all time. To be in his world . . . Mr. Brazell's acceptance was that important to me. At the very least, my sweeping brought me into a lair that I came to regard as a church—a tranquil place that I came to worship, just as I had with my own father when I was a little boy.

Mr. Brazell's garage also held another meaning. Paul had dubbed it "the command post" of the block. Over the years this garage became the place where the neighborhood men would converge and hold court after 3:00 P.M., while Paul's father would carry on with whatever project was at hand. No matter where Mr. Brazell was in his task, without breaking stride or without the need to make eye contact—as if he had his own unique radar—whenever a new shadow appeared to enter through the garage door, he never failed to offer a long *"hellooow . . ."* as his distinctive salutation.

The group seemed like a ensemble of characters from a television sitcom. There was Mr. Jolly, a robust, upbeat gentleman who worked selling sports equipment to the local schools and always let out a hacking cough whenever he fought to complete a sentence, while beads of sweat hung off his forehead. On a rare occasion David's father, Parker, joined the congregation as well as his next-door neighbor Mr. Ballow who, as a sign of affection, always seemed to haul off and smack his young son, Jake, on the side of his head. There was Amy's father, Mr. Neyland, who always eyed me with obvious suspicion. When I first came face-to-face with him, I had the perfect apology all planned out in my head, but in his presence and with the entire group suddenly hushed, my exasperated mumble made no sense to anyone, including myself. My next occasion to make my impression on Mr. Neyland and the other men was when I learned that Amy's father worked at the San Francisco airport. Having a passion for planes since I was small child, but without permission to break in and enter the conversation, I took a deep breath, locked onto Mr. Neyland's eyes, and blurted the most articulate statement my high-speed, air-filled mind could process: "Wow . . . planes! I like . . . how they, how they can fly!" From the back of the garage, Mr. Brazell suddenly lost his grip on a wrench and it clattered onto the cement floor, while someone behind me muttered, "And this is why tigers eat their young. Life in the food chain, gentlemen. I hear genius skips a generation. His father must have been Einstein."

The jab came from none other than my next-door neighbor, the self-proclaimed Guardian of Justice, Keeper of the Faith, Vietnam Veteran Extraordinaire, the Doc Savage of Duinsmoore: Michael A. Marsh, who sounded like the late movie star legend W. C. Fields and had the swagger and bravado of the high-strung "Gonzo" adventurous journalist Hunter S. Thompson of *Rolling Stone* magazine fame. No matter what diversion Paul, David, and I had planned for the afternoon, as soon as we saw "The Sarge" stroll over from his house to Mr. Brazell's garage with all the exertion of having just climbed Mount Everest, we'd cease activity and fight for any spot just beyond the fringes of the famed garage to eavesdrop. As compelling as the garage was, whenever Mr. Marsh appeared it suddenly jumped with excitement.

After hearing endless stories from Paul and David about the neighborhood legend and former special forces Vietnam War commando, I finally met Mr. Marsh one afternoon while trying to fix yet another massive oil leak from my minibike. Upon hearing the clattering sounds of a baby stroller, I looked up, wiping my grease-covered hand on my forehead, to see a tall man wearing a wide grin that was somehow holding onto a lit cigarette that dangled from his lower lip, a shrunken T-shirt with a plane circling a blue outlined cube that read *Fudpucker Airlines: We've been flying since the world's been square,* and a pair of faded shorts that exposed a pair of ash-white legs. With no apparent effort and without breaking stride, my neighbor was somehow able to push the stroller with one hand while taking gulps of beer with the other. "So *you're* the neighborhood threat? James Dean or Marlon Brando material you're not. But not to worry. Keep your chin up and your nose clean and we'll get along just fine." Before I could even think of a response from what I believed was another long list of endless put-downs, the man smiled before stating, "Good on you, boy! Get some!" he advised before moving on. All I could do was shake my head, thinking I must be going deaf and becoming immensely stupid, both at the same time, for I couldn't make out the meaning of what the Fudpucker man had just said. As Mr. Marsh disappeared down the street, I shook away any thoughts of being simpleminded, when I realized why should I care what some guy pushing a baby stroller thought of me.

The next afternoon while attempting to isolate yet another gaping leak from my mobile lawn mower engine, the Fudpucker man reappeared—at the same time, in the exact same outfit, with the same grin, with another lit cigarette glued to his lip, while clutching the stroller with one hand and protecting his precious Coors beer with the other. After another volley of one-liners, this time about "every dog having their day," he strolled on only to return thirty minutes later, to stop, gaze down, and state, "Perhaps introductions are in order. The name's Marsh. Michael Marsh." My ears suddenly perked up as Mr. Marsh somehow had the same rhythm and tone as my action hero, James Bond, whenever he introduced himself in the movies. Now *Mr. Marsh* suddenly captured *my* attention.

In a matter of days—and after Mr. Marsh's insistence that my hands and other body parts be sterilized and that I be on my best behavior—I was allowed to practically have free rein at "Marsh Manor," where I met his charming, subdued wife, Sandy, and their two children, William and Eric. While I adored both boys, it was Eric who, still a toddler, reminded me of my youngest brother, Kevin. I cherished Kevin to the point that I would risk extreme punishment if Mother ever caught me watching him crawling around in his blue jumper, let alone be with him in the same room. I'd stare in amazement at how Kevin made gurgling sounds while playing on the floor. But God help me if I ever socialized with my mother's children, since I was not a member of her family; only a prisoner. But now, at the Marsh's, I could, without fear of retribution, be on my hands and knees playing with Eric for hours upon endless hours.

Whenever the mood struck Mr. Marsh, who insisted that I address him as Mike, he'd drag out his tattered lawn chair, park it in front of his garage, then after raising a finger above his head as if taking a wind and a sun check, he'd peel off his shirt to bask in the late afternoon sun. After a few beers Mike would rattle off an endless array of episodes filled with high adventure about mountain climbing, war battles, or common everyday situations that only "The Sarge" could somehow make spellbinding. As the full cans of beers on his left side of his chair transformed into empty cans stacked into a pyramid on the right, Mike never skipped a beat. He'd continue to spin tales while reaching for a device that Mr. Brazell had made out of a heavy pipe attached to a worn gear and that Marsh would randomly seize and, without the aid of vision and as if squashing a bug, would snap down, flattening the aluminum beer can with a deafening thud. "Money in the bank, boy," Mike was known to inform. "The more I partake of the beverage of the gods, the more I am blessed through the powers of recycling. Mark my words, my young wards: Recycling . . . it's the future of America."

As much as I was amazed by Mike's silver tongue, staring at the endless rows of books—varying from European race cars, to movies and airplanes—was almost too much for me. As an elementary student I had devised a plan to help foil my mother's attempts to beat me by coming home with encyclopedia-sized books that my mind would devour in the bottom of the basement. Back then books were a form of escapism for me, and when one teacher suggested that I "read in between the lines," I strained my eyes to the point that I soon required glasses. Of all my subjects, I had loved planes the most. As a child I would fantasize that my arms could extend into wings and my legs into powerful jet engines with bright orange afterburners that would rocket me away from Mother's house, where I could fly high above any fear and toward the warmth of a never-setting sun.

"Heed these words, my young prodigy: knowledge is power. If you don't know, you won't know," Mike said the first time he caught me gawking at his library. "Welcome," he said while spreading his arms, "to the advanced institute of aeronautical studies. Choose wisely, young grasshopper, and study with diligence. The only rule is to leave the library as you found it. Borrow anything you wish, but replace thy tome when finished. *Capisce?*

"You're a young man with wide eyes and chicken-bone legs, and heaven help us all if we ever pry into that brain of yours. But not to worry, Slim. You've got something. All you need to do is find out what it is."

"Gentlemen," Mike announced that one afternoon in Mr. Brazell's garage when I had muttered to Mr. Neyland my embarrassing attempt at a sentence, "mark my words. My inspiring amigo, Señor Pel-zo, has the makings of greatness. The lad's destined to either save the world from peril . . . or be the cause of it."

"Kinda like Chuck Heston, from *Planet of the Apes*," someone countered.

"Exactly," Mike stated with an extended finger. "Which brings me to another point ..." Before stepping out from behind me and after giving me a firm tap on the shoulder, The Sarge, with his trademark Foster Grant sunglasses, cigarette dangling from his lower lip, and clutching a twelve-ounce aluminum cylinder of Coors, shook his head at me before stating the horrid conditions of our country's public schools. After nodding to others in the group, someone asked Mike about his day. After letting out a deep plume of smoke, then swallowing a fair portion of Coors, Mike replied, "Brother, let me tell ya. Life's a bitch and then you die. Only two things in life are certain: death and taxes. Life is a rat race and we're never gonna get out of it alive."

After a burst of chuckles from the men, my two friends and I stared at one another with utter amazement at how Mike said everything without the slightest effort. His words flowed like a stream of water. The Sarge then finished his beer and eyed his target before flinging the empty can and missing Mr. Brazell's garbage receptacle by a wide margin. Quick to recover, Mike stated, "You only live twice. Once when you're born and once when you stare death in the eye." Paul, David, and I didn't know what the hell he was saying, yet still shook our heads and let out a quiet *ah-ha* because he sounded so cool.

"So, Slim," Mr. Jolly laughed, "have you shot anybody today?"

As if performing his best John Wayne impersonation,

Mike leaned back and countered, "Let me tell ya, pilgrim. To you it's Goody . . . Slim Goody. Remember: Danger is no stranger to the Airborne Ranger. Shoot first, shoot last, and let God sort 'em out. Besides, my fellow nicotine-addicted friend, the day's not over yet!"

"Wow!" David said.

"Awesome!" I replied, shaking my head. "The guy's just too cool! I gotta write this stuff down!"

"When I'm old enough," Paul whispered, "I'm gonna join the army and be an Airborne Ranger just like The Sarge."

"Like, for sure." David shook his head. "Altar boys don't jump out of planes and shoot people."

About an hour later the group began to disperse. Tipping his can of beer at Mr. Brazell, Mike turned to leave but not before stopping in front of Howard and me with a final phrase of advice. "Remember: A man who loves whiskey and hates kids can't be all bad. There endeth the lesson of the day," The Sarge stated, emphasizing with a belch.

Again, not completely understanding Mike's language, all I could do was look at David Howard with wide eyes and exclaim, "Awesome!"

After school and on weekends I spent my time between whatever escapades Paul, David, and I could devise and peeking into Mr. Brazell's garage to hear the topic of the day and whatever tall tales The Sarge would spin for the amusement of his audience. Other times I'd escape to a corner of a room in the Marsh Manor and devour the words of one of Mike's books. Sometimes in the evening, after taking a shower at my foster home, I'd wipe off the condensation from the bathroom mirror to study my lips as I repeated whatever phrase I had heard from The Sarge, until I felt I had the timing and style down just right so as to impress Paul and David the following day.

Yet, however drawn I was to the adventurous, all-knowing, smooth-talking, hyper-thinking, musical connoisseur Mike—whose harmonious tastes varied from the guitar playing of Warren Zevon, to Leo Kottke, to the classical renderings of Gustav Holst's *The Planets*, to the lyrical satire of Leon Redbone's "Big Chief Buffalo Nickel"—in moments of calmness, within the evening stillness of the block, I'd slide open the Welshes' garage door to gaze over at Mr. Brazell working on one of his evening projects. Around Mr. Marsh at times I felt like a toddler running completely amok in a forbidden candy store, while in the presence of Mr. Brazell I became watchful and reserved, absorbing every detail as I once had with my own father when he labored in his work space.

One quiet overcast afternoon, during a rare reprieve from teenage chaos, I parked my minibike on its side before loitering within the confines of Mr. Brazell's garage. Mr. Brazell had just wiped his hands clean from his latest chore. "Well, hellooow, David." My black-framed glasses nearly flung up and over my head from snapping my neck backward so fast because Mr. Brazell had never greeted me with his trademark welcome. After placing a worn red rag on his workbench, Mr. Brazell strolled over and placed a hand on my shoulder. "I've been doing some thinking . . . and . . . after talking to Marsh . . . well . . . he tells me you're not the hellion you appear to be, even though Beth thinks . . . anyway, you don't need to stand around outside anymore. When I'm around you can just come on in." I began to shake my head while opening up my mouth to thank him when Mr. Brazell continued, "And quit calling me 'sir.' It's driving me crazy. From now on you can just call me 'Dan.' " With smiling eyes I extended my hand. "I was thinking," Dan said in a slow tone, "if you can afford the parts, I'd fix that minibike engine of yours . . . replace those . . . those gaskets, and the piston rings . . . and sand the valves down. . . . I have a little paint left over and some sandpaper. . . . If you'd take the time to sand down that bike frame of yours, well . . . I'd paint it for you . . . , if you want." Before I could say anything, Dan flashed a wide smile. "Of course with that bike of yours decommissioned for a few days, I'm sure there'll be less complaints from the neighbors."

For the next two weeks I ignored Paul and David, blazed through my homework and afternoon chores, shaving off any second possible, before tuning in my beat-up radio to the same station as Dan's from across the street. As meticulously as I could, I spread out a worn blanket that my foster father Mr. Welsh had used to pack some things when we moved, and with stacks of sandpaper carefully laid out according to grade, I began the never-ending task of taking each grade of sandpaper, rubbing back and forth until the grit and paper itself had worn off. After I completed the final stage of sanding, in which I used a gray sheet of wet sandpaper to remove the smallest flakes of paint, I proudly wheeled over my bike frame to show off to Dan. Immersed in one of his own projects and without taking a look at the frame, Dan simply probed, "How does it feel?"

Not understanding, I shook my head. With a slight sigh Dan strolled over, placing a gentle hand on my shoulder. "It looks good, but we can make it better. Here's what you do. Wash your hands. Make sure they're dry and as smooth as possible. Then, with your eyes closed, relax; and with the palm of your hand feel the frame. Just . . . feel the frame. When you pick up a bump or a chip, you'll know what to do. Some things are best trusted to a different sense."

I was beginning to understand and then he added, "I want you to go beyond what you think your standards are, what your capabilities are. Always accomplish a little more than you ever believed you could. I'm not just talking when it comes to the difference between a good mechanic and a great one, but everything you do in life go beyond, push yourself. Understand?" Dan finished with a nod.

Fours days later Dan inspected the bike frame by gently rubbing the tube, then smiling with approval. A short time later, after sweeping Dan's garage floor, he and I shared a moment alone. He sipped a beer while I nursed a can of Coke, both of us nodding without a word spoken, as we stared at the bare metal frame. Breaking the silence, Dan said, "You know, your engine's nearly rebuilt and if I can, I'll try to come home early from the shop tomorrow and see if I can paint the bike."

*   *   *

Two days later the stillness of the neighborhood was broken when I leaned over and with all my might pulled the starter to the engine. To my surprise the motor had a deep throaty sound and the coughing belching noise with all its blackened smoke was a thing of the past. With a wide grin glued to my face, and with Paul, David, and the group of men from Dan's garage surrounding my bright orange minibike, The Sarge held court, declaring the bike "Orange Crush" before anointing the bike with a few sprinkles of Coors. Mike then presented me with a sticker from his airline company that I proudly displayed on the handlebar section. After a mock salute from Dan, I ceremoniously rode around the neighborhood.

After a few cautionary laps around the block and paying close attention for any strange sounds while looking behind me for any oil leaks, I was becoming familiar with the bike's increased speed and instant response. Feeling comfortable with the bike, I turned my thoughts to the fantasy of finally beating Paul Brazell in a race. But my friend had a far more different, far more deviant, outlandish scheme. During the two-week lull in the pursuit of chaos, Paul, in a moment of boredom, had rediscovered his family's sixteen-millimeter camera. And now, as if a Hollywood director, with endless hand gestures and slinging out phrases such as camera angles, blocking, set-up shots, and fast-forward runs, Paul told David and I, in elaborate detail, his plans to make a James Bond–style film. Because I had the bright orange minibike that Paul stated would "pick up good on film" and a shiny, long Daisy barrel pellet gun, I would play the lead as Bond, while David was cast to play 007's demented yet fumbling nemesis, Dr. Strange. Going over every scene down to the second, Paul saved the climax of the film for last, in which Dr. Strange would somehow capture Bond's Super Top Secret "Use-Only-in-a-Crisis-to-Save-the-World" bike, then 007 in pursuit would catch up with Dr. Strange and jump on the moving bike before both men, while still on the minibike, would heroically—and as bloody and as long as possible—fight to the death. Then, after 007 somehow threw Dr. Strange off of the minibike, would the exhausted hero slip from the seat, becoming entangled with the fast-moving machine . . . and, at the last moment before getting killed from the bike, Bond, with blood dripping from his swollen face, would cringe with defeat before letting go of his precious vehicle, which would then explode into a million pieces. After Paul's elaborately detailed plans, he happily explained that there was only one problem: We had to choreograph every scene for one take.

As obsessed with adventure as I was, Paul's project gave me a few concerns. Yet while I kept probing Spielberg, Jr., with an endless stream of questions, my costar became so hyped-up that he insisted on staying "in character" as Dr. Strange, even though we had yet to film a single frame. The next morning, as soon as the sun's ray's burned off the morning mist, Paul and I on our minibikes set up a practice run at the end of the block for the film's climax. Thinking of everything, Paul had measured the street placing markers where Dr. Strange would seize the bike, where Bond would chase after him, and where Paul would be at every moment capturing everything on film. While Paul casually motored ahead, I gunned my throttle open and to my surprise the bike rocketed off. Upon reaching Paul's first set of markers, as instructed, I eased off the gas while Paul slid behind me for his predetermined camera shot. Everything seemed boringly perfect until I realized that my bike's throttle became jammed full open. After a few seconds, while I violently twisted the throttle back and forth trying to loosen its grip, to no avail, a panic attack began to take over when I discovered that by twisting the throttle I only made it open all the more. With Paul screaming for me to slow down, I raised my right hand, indicating everything was fine before bending down and lowering my arm to my emergency cutoff switch just above the engine's spark plug, which I immediately discovered would not cut off the engine. For some reason the more terrified I became, the faster the minibike seemed to pick up speed. With a quick prayer and taking a deep breath, I slammed down the heels of my tennis shoes, thinking *this* would take care of everything. When my shoes struck the pavement, the situation seemed under control. But as I held onto the hand grips while the smell of the rear tire spinning at supersoniclike speed burned my nostrils, I was concerned, for I had no idea what to do next. When I turned to look behind at the smoking tire, both shoes simultaneously lost their grip, the bike flipped forward, and all the while I maintained a death grip on the bike's throttle. When I realized my mistake, I saw the end of my shirt had become entangled in the rear wheel's sprocket and the side of my face was now only inches away from the same high-speed gear. With the rhythmic sounds of the engine's piston pumping away, the clanking of the newly greased chain, and the rear wheel spinning, in the back of my mind I just knew it was only a matter of seconds before the rear wheel's sprocket would catch my long shaggy hair, pull it in, followed by the entire side of my face sliced into thin strips, before the remainder of my skin would be fried like an egg on a grill when it came in contact with the engine's exhaust muffler. While my lower body flailed and my chest bounced on the seat of the bike, I could feel the heat from the exhaust fumes and a trickle of blood run down my forehead. Between every other bounce, my eyes locked onto a parked car in a driveway directly in front of me. Thinking it couldn't get worse, I tightened every muscle in my body before my fingers sprang free from the bike's hand grip.

With my hands outstretched and my twisted noodlelike body in midair, I felt like Superman—free of all the earthbound calamities, fighting for truth, justice, and the American way—until gravity and cold, hard mortal reality again took hold. Straining to keep my head up, my arms and knees broke my fall and absorbed the momentum, which was further reduced when I suddenly spread my arms and legs. My chin hitting the pavement became the final element to cease all rolling motion. Through tiny silver dots dancing in front of me, I could see my precious bright orange minibike barreling upright at full speed. I was proud

at how beautiful it looked and how perfect the engine performed. Then my eyes saw the bike hit the curve of the
sidewalk, jump up and over the back end of the parked car,
and disappear into a perfectly manicured bush. A second
later I heard an explosive "whoosh" as thousands of bright
green leaves shot into the air in the shape of a mushroom,
as if my bike had just set off a nuclear explosion.

From somewhere in the echoing distance I could hear
Dr. Strange laughing to no end. Moments later, Paul parked
his bike and jumped off, rambling, "That's it! That's *the*
shot. That's exactly, exactly what I'm looking for. Man,
Pelz, you take direction well. Now, let's do it again."

As David helped me up, I automatically checked my
limbs and the sides of my face. Feeling a warm sensation on
my knee, I limped over to the bomb site, leaned over, and
gently applied pressure to the strip of metal that made contact with the spark plug, which forced the engine to automatically sputter before losing all power.

On the advice of David, who was also the film's first-aid
technician, I took a day off to heal my wounds. And I was
overjoyed the next day when Paul's camera ran out of film
before filming "the ride of death" sequence. Even with the
demise of the film project I had been labeled "The Stunt
Master of Duinsmoore." Every day I did what I could to up
the ante, performing outrageous feats of human improba-
bility to fulfill my title. Yet over the weeks, endless scabs
healing on top of old ones, sets of broken glasses, multiple
burns, and torn clothes that I replaced with my dwindling
funds, I began to reevaluate my standing. With all that I

did as an adrenaline junkie, it never really escaped me that I was an older teenager, with only a few months to go before I was a legal adult and on my own. And as hard as I fought to push it all aside, I knew it was time for Peter Pan to grow up.

6

Moving On

In the middle of January of 1976, I reluctantly informed David Howard of the decision I had to make that had been gnawing at me for some time. "I gotta go," I stated in a broken, low voice.

"Hang on," David interrupted, "I'll grab my jacket and join ya. Let's get Paul."

"No, man," I countered, "you don't get it. I gotta move. I'm leaving."

David slumped his shoulders. "You're serious. You're not foolin'. . . . But why? What's up?"

I looked down at my grungy shoes and exhaled. "Well, I know I'm not gonna last much longer with the Welshes. It's just getting worse. They fight constantly. And it's just a matter of time before they call it quits. I've, like, seen this so many times before. . . . I'll get pulled one afternoon . . . so I might as well just push on now instead of being placed in Juve'e Hall."

"But how do you know? My parents go at it once in a

while when my dad's had too much to drink, so what's the deal?" I bowed my head down and away, refusing to answer. After a few seconds of silence David softly probed, "Do you know where you'll go? How many foster homes will this be?"

I stopped to count on my fingers all the different placements. "This will be my sixth family I've lived with. . . . And one home, the Turnboughs, I've lived in about three . . . no, make that four times. I'm hoping they'll take me in. If not, I'll end up in—"

"Juvenile Hall at Hillcrest?" David asked, knowing the answer. "But it doesn't make sense."

"Yeah, I know, it's just the way it is." I nodded. "It's happened before. I was with this one family and, well, they split up. Another time . . ." I paused. "Sometimes it just sucks. It's like as soon as I get used to things and maybe . . . maybe feel like I can fit in. . . ." I felt my frustration beginning to build and didn't want to get too much into my past in front of my friend. "The bottom line is I gotta go. I don't wanna, but I've got to move on."

"So," David sighed, "have you told Paul?"

I told him I had. "Sometimes talking to him is like trying to have a conversation with a rock. I can't read him. I don't know if he means to, but it's like he just doesn't care sometimes. When I said I was leaving he just nodded and looked right through me. Maybe he thinks I'm fooling around; I don't know. At least with you I know you're concerned. It's not like I've had a lot of close ties." I stopped to catch my breath before looking into David's eyes. "Can I tell you

something? I don't know how to read people. I have
idea what they mean when they look at me or say some
thing. Like at school, when they're teasing me, I don't
know if they're goofing around or really trying to tear me
up. At times I feel like such a doofus. I don't know who to
trust. A few years ago, I kept to myself. . . . I was by myself
a lot. That's why sometimes with Paul, I can't figure it out.
The only time I ever see him smile is when we're screwing around. Just so long as he doesn't get his minibike
scratched. . . ."

"Or he doesn't get hurt," David added.

"Or take the blame when we get busted," I added. "I
mean, don't get me wrong. I'm not trying to run him down.
I know I'm the screwball out of the bunch, and I know his
parents crack down on him, but it's like he thinks he lives
in a World War II Nazi prison camp. I just don't think Dan
or his mom treats him all that bad. So what's the deal?"

"Yeah, man," David chimed, "I see the same thing. Paul
just thinks everybody's on his case. He oughta deal with *my*
dad. . . ."

"Or *my mom!*" I cut in. "Again, I'm not running Paul
down and I'd die for him in a heartbeat, but I've been
through some serious and I mean serious shit with my own
family and lived with enough foster families to know
what's going on. I just don't think Paul knows how good he
has it."

"Paul can be a bit whiny and self-absorbed. . . ." David
continued. "Like, remember that time, at the park, when
you tried to light a fire at the barbecue pit?"

I nodded while my brain replayed the time when we were off from school during Christmas break. The three of us, as soon as we woke up, would head out to nearby Flood Park. While Paul and I raced each other on our minibikes on the narrow, paved sidewalk, David trailed behind on his bicycle until we met at our "super secret hideout," which amounted to a few scraggly bushes shielding a fire pit and a wooden picnic table and bench. *This* was our fortress of solitude. The three of us spent the morning hours as if we were grown-ups in Dan's garage standing by the lit barbecue pit rubbing our hands to keep us warm.

One cold dreary morning at the fortress, after David and I scoured the area for any dry twigs and leaves we could find, I sprayed them in the fire pit with a fair amount of lighter fluid from a can I had snatched from Mr. Welsh's garage. I was more afraid of the lit match going out that I held with the tips of my fingers than I was getting burned from a possible sudden fireball from the small puddle of lighter fluid. I carefully placed the match at the end of one of the small twigs. To my surprise a small flame ignited but, before it could catch, a chilling breeze blew it out. "Not enough fluid," Paul advised, shaking his head while sitting on his minibike. "More," David followed, "definitely more."

After three more attempts that ended with the same results and nearly depleting the entire can of lighter fluid, my frustration took hold as the chants from Paul and David went on nonstop. Trying to be witty, I bent over the fire pit with my last lit match and bellowed, "Here in my humble hand, I possess the eternal flame. A flame that will unite all of mankind. I propose that before the end of this decade all of mankind will become united. As a country we do these things; we do things not because they are easy but because they are hard," I stated as if I were President Kennedy making a monumental address. Before I could sing out a second verse, both friends yelled that my perpetual fire that would consolidate the masses of the world was about to fizzle out. Acting presidential, I quickly seized the can and squeezed its remainder into the dying fire. As I turned to Paul and David while my mind hummed "Hail to the Chief," I failed to notice a sudden blackish-orange flame that shot up in the air and nearly burned the side of my head. Nor was I concerned about the loud echoing "whoosh" noise that reverberated around me, for *President Dave did things not because they were easy but because he was obtuse.* As I continued to squeeze the last remaining droplets of fluid, a warm sensation ran from my right wrist all the way up the length of my arm. When I twirled around I saw to my horror a small stream of fire from the inferno fire pit arc in midair, until it reached not only the spout of the can but somehow my right arm as well. As Paul and David broke out in laughter, I nervously squeezed the can, only to feed the flame all the more. Thinking the can would instantly explode, taking me with it, my frantic mind telegraphed to my hand to let go of the can. Letting out a sound as if I were Curly of *The Three Stooges* in a prank that went awry, I flung the lit can up and over my right shoulder. A moment later, David used a handful of dirt he had scraped from the ground to put out my burning shirt. Before my heart could slow down, Paul suddenly let out a high-pitched yell. Thinking the worst, David and I turned to see a small stream of fire that licked the sides of Paul's mini-bike. In a flash Paul leaped up to the top of the wooden bench, grabbing my jacket and using it to beat away the flame. Within a few seconds, Paul's valiant effort saved his prized machine. "Damn, that was close," Paul huffed.

"Yeah," David agreed while he and I both stared at the burnt trail on my long-sleeved shirt, "that was a close one."

Replaying the story months later with David, it now seemed far more comical than before. "Man," David howled, "I've never seen Paul move so fast. 'My bike, my bike! Help me! Help me!'"

"Whoa! Whoa there, horsey! Talk about coming to my aid, what about you?" I asked jokingly. "What about the other time in the park? Remember?" I winked at David as I began reminding him of another "incident" at our favorite park.

That same winter, on the Sunday after Christmas, Paul, David, and I merrily strolled back to Duinsmoore after attempting to play with one of my presents: a gas-powered tethered airplane—which one had to constantly spin in a circle as the plane flew above the person, producing a high-pitched sound that made one's ears bleed until the person either collapsed from dizziness or an aneurysm. I lasted three revolutions. Afterward, as we left the small baseball field, I cradled my other Christmas gift, my ultimate prize:

a brand-new, no-frills tiny boom box, a combination AM/FM radio with cassette player, which I used to play my collection of Elton John tapes at all hours.

Regaining our hearing, David suggested we tinker with the airplane's fuel mixture, thinking the toy would fly higher and faster, and thus would be far easier to control as well as make less noise. While Paul rolled his eyes, Howard added, "What would happen if we revved up the plane, took off the string, and let it go?"

Suddenly Paul and I both stopped in our tracks. For a moment all I could do was stare at David. "With my luck, it would probably fly right into someone's head and shred them to death." For a moment I could see my cute little red airplane dive-bomb itself at Mrs. Brazell, or worse: straight into Amy's mother, Mrs. Neyland, right into her beehive hairdo.

"Come on," David urged trying to gain momentum. "We could launch it on the street from the house, like . . . like an aircraft carrier. Fly it up, let go of the string, and see what happens. It would be so cool! Come on, think of it, guys. The plane's buzzing down Duinsmoore, it spots Marsh's house, and does a kamikaze! Can you imagine The Sarge running out with his helmet on, yelling, 'Take cover! Incoming!'? He would so freak out!"

Loosening up, Paul joined in the twisted fantasy. "We could use our bikes and follow it like chase planes; like they do at NASA's test ranges. *Alpha, Whiskey, Tango, Delta. I have a visual. I have a visual.*"

"Yeah, we could watch it crash! *Uh oh, I can't hold it! I*

can't hold on! It's breaking up, it's breaking up! . . . But wait! We could rebuild it. We have the technology!" Paul salivated.

"I so cannot believe you're an altar boy. You, you heathen, devil child!" I scolded as if I were both Paul's and David's mothers. "Where did I go wrong?" I batted my eyes as if I were crying. "But officer, they were such good boys, quiet boys, practically angels, salt of the earth, the both of them. What's a mother to do?"

"Get a face-lift!" David shouted.

"Nose job!" Paul added.

"Boob job!" David screeched in perfect timing.

"Oh, what nasty, nasty boys!" I whimpered in a motherly voice before again thinking of my tiny red airplane screaming down the middle of Duinsmoore, while hundreds of folks scrambled in every direction. Although it had a twisted appeal, I told both friends that I'd have to think about it for a while. Besides, I informed them, the toy was a gift from my favorite foster mother, Mrs. Turnbough.

"Momma's boy! Momma's boy!" they both chanted at the top of their lungs, as we rounded a sharp corner and spotted a gang of older, tough-looking boys who were laughing as they passed around a funny-looking cigarette to each other. Thinking they failed to see us, and me having the experience of getting creamed at school for so long, I felt I knew how to get out of this. "Whatever you do," I whispered, "don't look at them. Walk backward and don't, I repeat, don't make a sound."

The three of us carefully retraced our steps with our heads bent down. After a few strides I thought that we might just escape, until the heel of my left foot snapped the only dry twig in the entire park. One of the boys who exhaled a cloud of smoke jerked his head up, locking onto my sweaty face. As if stalking their prey, the group of boys slowly formed a close circle around me. As I turned to look behind me, I could see Paul and David were magically outside the perimeter of danger. Before I could fire off for my two friends to come and help defend me, the tallest boy snarled, "Ay, that's one fine 'box' you got there."

Suddenly feeling less apprehensive, I smiled, "Why thank you, sir. I'm sure you could get one at Kmart or any other fine department store."

"Could get one now." The boy smiled back before taking another drag. "Now, give me that tune box. Give it up!" he ordered, taking a dramatic step forward.

As the bully approached me I took a step backward, bumping into one of his friends, who shoved me back toward their leader. Still thinking I could reason with the bully, whom I now realized had bulging arms, I thrust my red airplane into his face. "Here, take this! It's motorized! It flies and provides hours of endless entertainment!"

A second later I felt a pythonlike grip squeezing my neck. "I've seen you at school. I know who you are. Give it up, man, and walk away. Just walk away." The more I tightened my grip around the handle of my radio that contained my favorite Elton John tape, the more the bully seemed to coil his arm. As I began to feel lightheaded, I thought for sure that Paul and David would jump in any second and rescue me from certain death. A few seconds later I woke up on the ground to see the leader of the gang thrust my radio high into the air. I stood up, marched up to him, and pleaded with him to give me back my radio. "*Your* radio?" the bully chanted before tossing it over my head to another boy, then to another and another. As I tried to leap up and snatch back my boom box, a stinging blow hit the side of my head. "Just don't listen, do ya?" the leader hissed.

"But it's *my* radio. Not yours, but mine!" I yelled back as I closed my hands into a pair of fists.

"Don't matter none. And now I gots to take you down. Gots to teach you a lesson," he said while extending his arms and curling his fingers and looking exactly like the kung fu legend Bruce Lee.

I flashed "Bruce Lee" a nervous smile before uttering "Oh, shit!" He then bowed his head slightly, gave me a sly smile in return, twisted at the hips as if about to turn away before his right leg sprang up and his foot struck me in the middle of my face. A second later I could feel my head jerk backward as my glasses flew through the air. The moment my body fell back on the dirt, the gang of boys took turns kicking me from all sides. Learning from the endless stompings at school, I developed a technique of defending myself—absorb any blows by curling up into a ball, while praying no one would step on my glasses.

But that was *my* radio. I knew it was a cheap, no-name-brand boom box whose batteries barely lasted an hour and whose cassette device always seemed to drag my tapes until I hauled off and smacked the radio on its side. When it came to dealing with others my age, as always I knew I didn't fit in at school. But big deal, I had told myself some time ago that half of what I saw at high school was idiotic social posturing. Getting my legs kicked out from behind me, forcing me to drop to my knees and scramble around to find my books was an elementary school prank. At Menlo-Atherton High School, the first time someone came from behind me and went through my pockets while I was standing up going to the bathroom was the last time I allowed myself to be that vulnerable. I could not prevent what others thought about me or how they treated me. On the outside I appeared to be a gullible, easy mark, but what others failed to recognize was that beyond the depths of my skin was a deep well of motivational reserve. I came to believe that if I could survive living with my mother and all that went with it, then I could probably overcome whatever life threw my way.

So I yelled at myself to get up. Then without thinking of the repercussions, I snuck over to the bully, somehow snatched back my radio, then took off so fast that I thought I was running on air.

When I reached the parking lot, to my surprise John Welsh's golden Chrysler Fury bounced high into the air as he drove over the speed bumps in triple-digit haste. It took another full second for me to discover David Howard sitting beside Mr. Welsh and grinning from ear to ear.

"Man," David huffed while shaking his head, "I almost forgot about that day. I thought for sure those guys were gonna kill you. You had bruises on your head for a week, remember?"

"Remember? What about that oath of brotherhood we took in Dan's garage? Like, when one of us is in trouble the others will help out?" I jokingly asked David.

"Man, don't look at me. Paul said that, not me. But I gotta tell ya, when those dudes were beating you up, I asked Paul if he wanted to jump in, and he says, and I'm not kidding, he says, 'Nah, Pelz is doing just fine.' Paul just chickened out. But hey, at least we ran home and got the cavalry!"

"That was very much appreciated," I said before thinking how John Welsh, Howard, and I then crossed over the bridge that led to what we dubbed "The DMZ," as we searched for the gang who jumped me. When my foster father spotted a group of older boys standing around a porch, he skidded the car to a stop and jumped out carrying an axe handle, while I hovered beside him, trying to act tough even though I was so close to relieving myself.

"And if memory serves," I again chided my friend, "you opened the car door brandishing a pair of . . . what? John's drumsticks? . . . before slamming the door shut and locking yourself inside?"

"I got a pretty face," David smiled before changing the subject, saving himself from certain ridicule. "Hey!" Howard almost yelled, "How 'bout that time, what was it . . . last week, when we launched that rocket engine?"

"I thought for sure Mr. Neyland would find me and kick my behind," I stated with fear as I recalled another playful diversion that had gone completely awry. At the end of a lazy weekend, as I cleaned out a box of old toys, I came across an abandoned model rocket engine. I casually showed it to Paul, the whiz kid of the group, and David, and together, the three of us thought it would be *interesting* to see what would happen if we taped the cigar-shaped engine to a lightweight four-wheeled toy. Would the thrust of the monstrous motor make the toy lurch into the air and fly away? Or would it simply stand still and do nothing? Or just maybe it would rocket down the street so fast that it would break the sound barrier, creating a *Star Trek*–like "worm hole," sucking the three of us into another dimension? After digging through another box of my baby foster brother's unwanted toys, I found a small plastic yellow tractor with a man proudly perched in the driver's seat. We immediately called the toy "Farmer Joe." When David assured me that the length of the street was clear, I carefully leaned over to light the engine, thinking of what happened to my arm the last time I held a match in my hand. When the makeshift fuse was lit I proudly yelled out, "Fire in the hole!" a split second before a small, dark, orange-yellow flame spewed from the back of the toy tractor. As Farmer Joe sped away at Mach–like speed, something near the end of the block suddenly jumped out into the middle of the street. Through a cloud of brown smoke from Joe's exhaust, I could see the object itself was none other than the Shirley Temple of Duinsmoore Way, little Amy Neyland. And, as if a possessed heat-seeking missile, Farmer Joe headed directly toward its target.

The three of us snapped our heads at one another in disbelief before waving our arms, signaling for Amy to step aside. We only confused the little girl all the more by flailing our arms in different directions. Sensing imminent danger, Amy wisely sidestepped out of the missile's path. But Farmer Joe, as if advancing into "target acquisition mode," adjusted its flight path toward Amy. When Paul, David, and I gestured for Amy to step in the opposite direction, the plastic tractor's wheels skipped for a moment, before readjusting its trajectory to Amy.

Now I was worried. What Paul and David didn't know, what I kept to myself as a climactic, dramatic surprise was, before attaching the rocket engine to Farmer Joe, I had deliberately crimped the end of the engine, knowing the engine would explode when it reached its end. In my mind I could imagine sweet little Amy sidestepping back and forth as if she were square-dancing, as the runaway missile maintained its target lock and before detonating, burning Amy's hair, singeing her clothes, or worse, causing instant decapitation and loss of limbs. In the middle of the street I suddenly dropped to the pavement and covered my head in anticipation of any fallout while chanting, "Jesus, God! Jesus, God! Don't explode. Don't explode!" After a few seconds I opened my eyes and removed my hands from the sides of my face, expecting the worst. Beside me, Paul and Howard stood roaring with laughter. After a few squints I could see that Farmer Joe had stopped several feet in front of Amy, in one piece.

* * *

"You really thought that Farmer Joe would blow up?" Howard asked.

"Not a doubt in my mind," I responded. "I got lucky."

"Man, we did some crazy stuff," David stated.

"Yeah," I nodded, "but, I gotta go."

"But why? Why do you have to leave?"

"You just don't get it. The deal is, once a foster kid turns eighteen, they 'age out'—out of the system. I'll be on my own. So whatever money I've saved at that time is all I'll have when I'm on my own. I'll tell you one thing: I'm not gonna be homeless or go hungry. No way, not me. I'm gonna do whatever I can to make sure that doesn't happen."

Howard shook his head in disagreement. "Dude, chill out! You're too paranoid. That's years away."

I could feel my entire body tense up. "I'm not being paranoid. I just turned fifteen. Do you know what that means? I've got less then three years and that ain't a lot of time. Do you know how much an apartment goes for? It's anywhere from three to five hundred dollars a month. And, that's for a run-down, unfurnished studio. I've checked it out. They want first and last months' rent up front. My last job as a busboy, they started me out at $1.65 an hour. At my last burger joint I worked for I thought I was Rockefeller when I got a raise that paid me $2.65. You do the math. I've got to get back to work. I've got to get a couple of jobs!"

David playfully punched my arm. "It's no big deal. You'll be fine."

Without intending to, I lashed out at my friend. "It *is* a

big deal! You think I wanna end up like some of the other guys I knew who 'aged out,' or . . . end up like my dad?"

David simply stared at me with an open mouth.

"I'm sorry, man," I apologized. "I didn't mean to blow a gasket."

"I understand about aging out; that's cool. But what's this about your dad?" David quietly asked.

"My parents," I began, "well, they drank a lot. They're, uh, both alcoholics. My mom, well, she'd get hammered and would go off on me. It was pretty bad; that's why I'm in foster care. . . ."

Howard's eyes grew wide as he interrupted, "Man, why didn't you run away or fight back?"

I turned away from David's piercing stare. "It's a long story. Anyway, it all started before kindergarten. Back then I thought it was normal to be treated that way. By the time I realized what was going on, I was too scared to do anything. Don't get me wrong; my dad never did anything to me. At first I thought it was the booze that drove my mom past the edge, and as a kid I used to fantasize that if she got sober, my mom would like just wake up, realize all the crap she did before, and she'd make up to me, and we'd be The Brady Bunch forever. But it just got to the point I had to survive any way I could."

"Man, that's some sick shit. But your dad; didn't you tell me once that he's a firefighter up north in Frisco? Why didn't he do anything?"

I let out a deep sigh. The last thing I wanted to do in

front of David, another guy, was open up my past and cry like a baby.

"Come on, man, it's cool, you can tell me."

"My dad," I paused, "my dad was a drunk who wasn't there a lot and really didn't know what was going on." As the words spilled out I quickly covered my mouth when I realized I had uttered out loud 'my dad was a drunk.' "When I was either nine or ten, he told me he wasn't going to put up with it much longer. *'The next time she throws you down the stairs . . . the next time she starves you . . . the next time she has you swallow ammonia . . . I'm not gonna put up with that . . . the next time. . . .'* " I paraphrased in a deep fatherlylike voice.

"Swallowed ammonia!" David shrieked.

I waited a few seconds before nodding my head. "Yeah, twice. The second time was in front of my dad. The thing is, you can't breathe. It's that quick!" I said, snapping my fingers. "So, I'm on my knees, trying to force this, this invisible air bubble out so I can breathe, and I remember staring at my father's shoes. They were black and not a scuff mark on them, just a few inches in front of me. And all he did was stare down at me as if I were some kind of animal. He used to 'negotiate' with my mom, but I dunno, over time and all that booze . . . he never stopped my mom. And neither did I."

"You swallowed ammonia? No way," David repeated.

"Promise you won't say anything to anyone, even to Paul? I don't want anyone to know," I said in a soft voice.

David gave me a nod. With my eyes darting in both directions to make certain that no one was nearby, I then opened my mouth and exposed my discolored tongue.

Howard leaned forward, inspecting it, before uttering, "Dude, that's gross."

"Anyway," I said, cutting off David and wanting to flee the subject before I totally lost it, I continued, "back in '73 I had just turned twelve, and a couple weeks into January my mom basically loads my four brothers and me into her beat-up station wagon and takes us to this run-down area in San Fran. She gives my dad this cardboard box with all this stuff. You get it, man? A box—his entire life in a box. I remember trying to breathe in, to suck in his cologne. I think it was Old Spice. I just wanted to . . . to hang on to . . . something that was his. And my mom wouldn't let me look at him. So, as my mom drives off, I turn to steal a glance at my dad and here's this guy, this guy who rescues kids from burning buildings, and . . . and, uh . . . he can't even save himself. Imagine that's you standing in the rain, drenched to the bone, watching your world drive away. You think that doesn't stick with ya?

"When it comes to what happened, sometimes I just don't know what to make of it. Sometimes I feel like I'm going to lose it, but it passes and I try to keep it together. I know I'm an idiot, but I also know this: I don't ever want to end up not knowing where my next meal's coming from."

Glancing back up at David, I could see a tiny stream run from his eyes. "Why do some people hate so much?"

"I dunno," I said, shaking my head. "I used to think

about my mom and I can't figure it out. I mean, look at the Middle East. Every time I turn on the news, there's all this killing. Over there, like across the bridge at the DMZ, they've been so pissed off at whatever for so long that after a while they forget why. They just know they hate. Marsh says Iran's gonna be the next big thing. Those folks over there, they hate the shah.

"I mean, look at Hitler and all the sick shit he did. Do you know how many millions upon millions of people died on both sides of the war, just because of this one guy's hatred?"

David nodded. "I read in school that he was abused as a kid. . . ."

I waved my hand in front of my friend. "I don't buy that. It may have been true, but it's just an excuse. That doesn't give him the right to do what he did. I'm not trying to run anyone down, but I can't tell you, David, how many foster kids I been with or these tough guys I see in Juve'e Hall who use whatever happened to them as an excuse for anything *they've* done, or how they think they can, like, milk it for the rest of their lives. Just because of some shit from their past. It's like if they hate so much, maybe they figure no one will ever hurt them again. But like I said, I think they hate so hard for so long that they forget what made them that way. I don't know how I feel about what all my mom did to me. I just know I don't want to end up like her or my dad. That's why I gotta maintain my focus. I gotta go. You get it now, man?"

David bowed his head before nodding in agreement.

"Maybe you could live here with me. We could, like, share my room. Think of it. It'd be so cool. We could be like brothers."

Without thinking, I took David's hand. "Thanks, I really appreciate it. But if I stay here, I know what's gonna happen. I'm just going to goof off until one day I wake up and *bam:* I'm eighteen and out on my own without a stake. I've gotta move on and grow up—hunker down, keep that nose to the grindstone, and apply a little elbow grease!—I said, imitating The Sarge during one of his endless "take on some responsibility" sermons.

"Come on, David, cheer up! It's not like I'm not ever going to see you guys again. Mike and his wife, Sandy, said I could crash at their place on the weekends. Me leaving doesn't change a thing. We're still brothers!"

David smiled back. "Brothers," he announced.

Trying to break the tension, I added, "I look at it this way: Living here, getting to know you and Paul, and all the stuff we did together was the time of my life. It was like, like, Disneyland for incorrigibles."

David and I then walked around the block after stopping at Paul's and trying to pry him out of his room. After much pleading from David and me, Paul decided to remain inside, so my friend and I took one last stroll together for the last time.

The next Saturday Mr. Turnbough—my former and now final foster father—helped me load my belongings into his ancient grayish-blue and white Chevrolet pickup truck. Before driving away, my two friends and I tried to play it cool and act as if my departure was no big deal, until David leaned over to give me a quick hug, while Paul perched on his minibike, acknowledged me with a nod. As I closed the door to Mr. Turnbough's truck, my eyes caught sight of Dan, who had momentarily stepped out from his lair, giving me a mock salute with one of his gleaming wrenches.

As I motored away, my fingers tapped on a set of books The Sarge had given me, along with his stern encouragement to "keep the faith" and "persevere at all cost." Leaning back on the worn bench seat, my mind flashed back to the endless stream of adventures I had had in the last four months since moving to Duinsmoore Way. For me, it was never pushing our misguided shenanigans to the limits, but the constant exploration of an everyday world that I cherished in amazement. Paul, David, and I knew that at any moment of any day something wonderful, something magical, could suddenly happen, and the three of us would take part in it. And, for the first time, I didn't overanalyze. I didn't hold back or instantly retreat deep within my inner shell. For years, feeling inferior about myself also provided the perfect cocoon. I did it all and relished every moment. To me, Duinsmoore Way was Disneyland . . . and I couldn't wait to return to the "Happiest Place on Earth."

7

Girl World

Within weeks of moving back in with the Turnbough family, I fell into my pre-Duinsmoore routine of barely applying myself at high school, while my sole intention was to obtain any and all menial jobs I could find. More than ever my mind-set was that school was a place that stole precious time away from me trying to earn a living. I strongly believed that history, science, English, and especially learning fractions in math had no practical applications in the "real world." Over the months, the drive to apply myself declined to the point where, after scanning through what project lay on my school desk, I'd daydream of Duinsmoore and cover my head, and pass out from exhaustion from working yet another lengthy shift at the local plastics factory.

As the months passed into different seasons, I became more robotic than before. I would shave any second possible by checking my weekly work calendar pinned to my bedroom wall, frantically peeling off my school clothes and scurrying off to work. Yet, twice a month, no matter how much grime stuck to my tattered work clothes, face, or matted hair, I'd proudly march into the bank, carefully unfold my crumpled check, and empty my pockets of any loose change I had received from any of my odd jobs. I would then triumphantly stroll out with my head held high, calculating my worldly savings with a seven percent interest rate.

After work when I walked home at night, I'd stroll through the streets seeing the rusted-out cars resting on worn cinder blocks and homes where the only activity came from blaring television sets. During the day, while some neighborhoods had a few kids riding bikes or playing outside, none had a sense of community. I'd sometimes deviate from my direct route and search for that one street or even part of a neighborhood that formed my idea of a happy neighborhood. While some were well groomed and others seemed to have a sense of togetherness, I felt that nothing came close to the magic of Duinsmoore Way.

On a rare weekend off, I easily convinced the Turnboughs before pestering Mike and Sandy Marsh to allow me to stay with their family for a few days. After catching a shuttle bus to the nearby airport, I caught a ride with The Sarge as he drove home from work while he rattled off diatribes—the plight of the working man, greedy corporate management, taxation without proper representation, and scandalous, no-good, no-sense, scum-sucking politicians or third world countries running amok. After Mike blew off some steam, I realized that when it was just the two of us, he acted more like a concerned uncle than a performing comedian. As he piloted his red Toyota SR-5 hatchback into Duinsmoore, I felt like an excited puppy with my nose plastered against the window. Before Mike could apply his parking brake, I had disappeared from his sight, running into the middle of the street to find David. He saw me immediately and ran over to give me a quick hug.

We wasted no time with the small talk. With wide, smiling eyes David asked after our embrace, "What ya got planned?"

"I dunno," I said with glee, "I just got here. But we've got to do *something!* Let's get Paul!" While David and I strolled on the new redbrick walkway that Dan laid leading to their house, we both jabbered away interrupting each other. After rapping on the screen door, Paul answered, acting as if we had just woke him from a nap. "Hey!" I exclaimed, "I'm here for the weekend! Let's go do something!"

"Well, I don't know. I'm kinda busy," Paul said, shrugging his shoulders.

"Doin' what?" David countered.

"You know . . . stuff," Paul mumbled.

"Come on!" I said, nearly jumping out of my skin from enthusiasm. "I haven't seen you in months! We'll go to the park, we'll goof around. Come on, let's hang."

Seconds slipped away, then Paul said, "Well," while rubbing the back of his neck, "when you guys know what you're gonna do, come over and get me."

Without meaning to, I let out a sarcastic sigh in front of Paul before turning away. After a few paces I asked, "Man, what the hell's up with Paul?"

"Dude," David said as he gave me a pat on the back, "that's Paul. Sometimes he gets withdrawn and I won't see him for weeks. Forget him. Let's take a walk." The next half hour David and I could barely shuffle our feet forward as I was absorbing every scent and capturing any slight nuances of the neighborhood. Finishing the walk, David and I stopped in front of Mr. Brazell's garage, which was already filled with the usual group. Feeling unsure I cautiously hovered outside until Dan spotted me, and he walked over, smiling. "Hellooow, David."

After shaking hands, I stood with David by Dan's workbench, taking in the scene. Nothing seemed to change. The Sarge regaled us with tall tales while clutching his beer, the street was littered with laughing children, and the entire block maintained its immaculate crispness.

As the months passed, I savored my weekend visits, bunking at either the Marshes', David's, or Paul's house. One weekend while staying at David's, he and I spent the majority of the day listening to his Captain and Tennille record. After hearing the record for the umpteenth time I jokingly stated, "Man, this is worse than . . . what was the name of that song . . . 'Wild Fire'? What the hell is 'Muskrat Love' anyway? I tell ya, Tennille, she's a fox, but I don't see how love's gonna keep *them* together."

"Dude," David whimpered in a fake cry, "I'm a sensitive guy. How can you say that? You know I love Tennille."

"Why can't they call it 'Foxy Love'? Check it out: *A hunk, a hunka foxy love. A hunka, hunka foxy love,*" I crooned, imitating Elvis Presley and ending with, "Thank ya, thank ya vary much. Momma, momma, I's ready for another deep-fried peanut butter sandwich. 'Cilla, Priscilla. Woman, where the hell you at? Daddy needs a foot rub."

"You like Elvis?" David gasped. "He is sooo uncool."

"Man," I said shaking my head in mock disgust, "I thought you said you was a sensitive guy? The King's okay. My foster sister, Nancy, goes gaga over this guy. Every time he's on TV and wiggles his hips or legs, it's like she's gonna faint. What's up with that? I don't see anyone fainting over the Captain. Tennille, now she's a fox, but the Captain, he has so got to go!"

"Agreed," David huffed. "But if you want to know why girls go crazy for guys like Elvis, you have got to check this out," David said before leaping up from his bed to ensure his door was closed and locked. Then, to not set off the "Parent Detector," he tiptoed back to the bed, lifted up a corner of his mattress, and pulled out a thin worn book.

Doing my best to scare David, I breathed in, acting as if I were going to screech, but instead said mockingly, "Why, David Howard, what do you have in your filthy little hands?"

"Dude, shut up! My sister's in the next room!" David warned as he ceremoniously laid out the book on his bed.

"Wow!" I exhaled, "this is too cool! Can I touch it?"

With his arms crossed on his chest David nodded. "Be my guest."

"Man, I heard about stuff like this before, but I never thought . . . Wow!" I quickly snatched the book frantically scanning the pages for any photos before uttering the title aloud, *"How to Pick up Girls.* Too cool. This is James Bond cool. Does it work?"

David cracked a wide smile. "What do you think?"

Looking at his thinly veiled poker face, I knew David wanted me to believe that this magical book would unleash the awe and mystery of the world of girls. Looking at David, I knew he was overplaying his hand. He was no Casanova. "So, does it work?"

"You'll just have to find out," he snorted.

"Maybe I'll try some moves on Paul's sister, Dori, or maybe even your sister, Sharon," I said, raising my eyebrows.

"Now Dori I can understand, but my sister, Sharon, that's gross," David countered, wiping his hand against his mouth. "Hey, maybe you could read the book and, like, try out some stuff on your foster sisters!"

"That's even grosser!" I fired back while again scanning through the text.

"Hey, Pelz," David whispered, "have you like, walked in on any of your foster sisters while they're naked in the shower all lathered with soapy bubbles?"

Closing the book, I looked up at David. "No," I said in a whisper, but there was this one time . . ." I lowered my voice even more, while David scooted over closer to me. "Once, when I was walking down the hallway at the Turnboughs' house, my foster sister, Nancy, had her door cracked open, and I turned 'cause I could hear Elvis blaring from her stereo. And for a second, one everlasting Kodak moment, I saw Nancy fling off her bra. And man, I saw everything."

"Everything?" David repeated.

"Yep." I shook my head. "Everything."

"Awesome." David nodded while rubbing his hands. "You got to see a real live girl. How did it feel?"

"Kinda weird," I answered. "I was scared 'cause you know you're sneakin' a peek, but you're kinda excited at the same time." Switching focus I asked, "So . . . have you ever seen a girl naked? And I don't mean your sister, or your mom, or sneaking into an R-rated movie, but a real, *real* girl?"

Huddled close together, David spoke in a much lower voice. "I don't know if you know, but my parents own the house next door; not the Ballows' but the other side. Anyway, these teachers live there, a whole school of them. Get it?! *A school of teachers.*"

"Come on, man!" I hissed, "get to the good stuff."

"On weekends they'd all hang out in the backyard. And I built this small stand in the middle of these bushes so I could peek over, and, uh, anyway, I watched them sunbathe topless, for hours. They'd be giggling, rolling over, putting suntan lotion on each others' backs."

"Cool," I nodded, "too cool. Man, next time I wanna be with you and check it out."

"No can do," David said, shaking his head. "They all moved out."

"What a rip-off."

"So," David said after a moment of pause, while another

rendition of "Muskrat Love" echoed in the small room, "have you ever done it? You know, gone all the way?"

The shy feelings and ickiness I felt about a subject people didn't like to speak about, or even rarely acknowledge, began to fade, and soon it was like my best friend and I were simply chatting about the weather.

"Well," I stated, opening up to David all the more, "I almost kissed a girl. And I don't mean no peck on the cheek thing but a real full-blown kiss." I told David the story about the time we were moving into Duinsmoore, when I sauntered up the street to meet an incredible-looking girl who had glanced over before winking at me, while I helped Mr. Welsh with the last of the belongings from the U-Haul.

The second I saw the young lady, I sucked in my chest, covered by a soiled, faded tank top, so she would never know how skinny I truly was, while I stood on my toes, hoping to impress that my height meant I was years older and much more mature—a man of experience. Keeping my nervousness under control, I repeated to myself, *Bond, James Bond*. Giggling at my lame attempts, the girl flashed a wide smile followed by a long wink, then sashayed away. Realizing this was a moment of a lifetime, it only took a mere heartbeat for me to ditch Mr. Welsh and rush over to Paul who had miraculously witnessed the entire episode.

Giving me a sly nod, Paul, one of my new friends, had a simple plan: Go ahead and meet this girl. But as excited as I was, and with a thousand thoughts racing through my head, I didn't have the guts to do it. Just months before, strolling down a crowded school hallway between classes and lifting my head to make eye contact with the first girl I saw was too much for me. While everyone else seemingly had wild times, partied, and "went all the way" on Friday nights, I, on the other hand, planted myself in front of the TV breathlessly waiting to watch *The Donny & Marie Show*.

And yet I couldn't open up to Paul and tell him how I thought about myself. To Paul and David, I was a pencil-thin, four-eyed rebel version of James Dean. Paul didn't care. Without hesitation he gave me his best long-sleeved shirt to wear that would surely impress the maiden: a red-and-black checkered flannel, which, I discovered to my horror, had the sleeve stop just past my elbow. "I'm gonna look like a geek!"

"She won't notice!" Paul retorted.

"I thought you just said 'girls like sharp-dressed guys'?"

"Forget what I just said and go meet her!" Paul ordered. "Go!"

"All right," I yelled back, "if you quit being an old hen for a moment, I can, ya know, get my thoughts to-gether. . . ." I was scared, not because I was terrified of girls or that I had never had any contact with girls besides my foster sisters, but because of how absolutely inferior I felt about myself. Whenever I glanced at the mirror I detested what stared back at me. I made certain whenever I brushed my teeth or combed my hair that my eyes never gazed too long at the reflective glass. "Okay," I said after emptying my lungs, "what do I say?"

Shaking his head in disappointment, Paul advised,

"Well, whatever you do, don't say anything stupid." Paul said with a snap of his fingers, "Just come up with a smooth one-liner like they do in the movies."

I instantly thought of Cary Grant, the suave, sharp-dressed, well-versed actor. *"Judy, Judy, Judy. Tell me, how's a girl like you get to be a girl like you?"* No, I corrected myself, unless she was an avid moviegoer she would definitely think I was way too weird. But, I said to myself, there was always, ol' 007. I could imagine casually strolling up to her and introducing myself by confidently stating, *Pelzer . . . Dave Pelzer.* But since I had more crater-sized pimples than the surface of the moon and wore paint-stained, chipped, thick black-framed glasses and had not one iota of sex appeal, I quickly shelved that idea. All I could do was thank Paul and pray to God that I didn't make a complete spaz of myself in the next few minutes.

Leaving Paul's house and walking up the street to the other block, I felt surprisingly calm. Here I was strolling down one of the most beautiful neighborhoods in the world, about to meet an incredible-looking girl who actually seemed interested in *me!* Taking my time, my eyes became a camera, snapping shots of the endless array of bright flowers that complemented nearly every home. My ears picked up the slightest sound of thousands of leaves rustling from a gentle breeze. Passing a house, I paused to draw in a lungful of jasmine, hoping my clothes would absorb the sweet smell. Whatever burdens from my past or everyday dilemmas that at times seemed to cling to me like barnacles all suddenly fell away. For a moment, I felt ten feet tall. Today was an extraordinary day.

I had no idea what I was going to say. I had no thought-provoking, quick-witted one-liners *and* I didn't care. If she liked me, great. And if she didn't, well, I knew it wasn't the end of the world. On the outside I knew how awkward I was. I only hoped she could see past that and see me for the person I was within. As I approached the house, I threw my shoulders back, raised my chin, smelled my breath, and checked my armpits for any odor. After tapping on the door in a light but confident manner, I stepped back, held my hands behind my back and waited. And waited. And waited. And waited. My poise became Jell-O as my mind began to spin into overdrive, contemplating various scenarios—maybe I was at the wrong house, the wrong block. Maybe she saw me and hated what I wore. Maybe she found out I was a total geek. Or, maybe this was another in a long string of sick jokes that I played into yet again. The longer I stayed at the front of the door, the longer I felt everyone in the world was staring at me. I could feel tiny beads of moisture collect on the palms of my hands. It was time to flee.

Without warning the door suddenly burst open. Startled, I jumped backward, landing on my knee, but of course I acted as if I had just dropped something of no importance on the ground and casually found it. Gazing up I swallowed hard, hoping she didn't hear me gulp.

"Hey," she cooed as my eyes tracked her body from her toes to her nose. I simply nodded as if I were mute. The girl matched my gesture before stating in a louder voice. *"I'm Debbie."*

With my brain locked, my mouth muttered, "Deb ... Debbie," as if I were Tarzan mimicking Jane's pronunciation. By luck, the moment the word stuttered out, my body began to lock up as my brain screamed, *"You idiot! What the hell are you doing? Wake up! Say something, anything!"*

Taking a deep breath through my nose, my sudden tension began to subside. Standing up, I tilted my head slightly, stared at the side of her face, squinted my right eye as if from the sun's glare, and in a slow groveling voice announced, "I was ... in the neighborhood and figured I'd stop by and say ... hello."

Debbie's eyes suddenly blinked as her nostrils flared. I squinted my other eye while giving Debbie a slight nod as if I were disclosing some unknown mystery through the wonder of body language. I didn't have the vaguest idea of what the hell I was doing, but my confidence suddenly soared. As my stance became more relaxed, I found myself talking to Debbie in a soft, low voice, which forced her to lean closer. I could almost taste the sweet scent from Debbie's perfume that seemed to rise from the bottom part of her neck. I quickly learned the more Debbie spoke, the less I had to struggle to impress her with witty banter, which saved me all the more from uttering something moronic. Then when Debbie finished with her remarks, I'd give her a slight nod or subtle laugh. Even though I could hear everything Debbie said, my mind ran off in a million different directions. I rattled off a few one-liners as if I were James

Bond, Clint Eastwood, and the infamous Sarge all in one. But surprisingly, they were my thoughts and my words. The more the words flowed out, I smiled at myself, thinking how easy it was to make Debbie smile. I never thought talking to a girl would be so effortless.

Then I saw it. The move. It took me a few seconds, but I suddenly realized when I finally quit jabbering away, as if to come up for air, Debbie leaned over, flicked the tip of her tongue through parted lips before gently closing her eyes. Having never had the opportunity to be this close to a mature girl before, I stared directly at her face. The bangs of Debbie's hair were perfectly curled under. The ends of her thickened eyebrows were a little clumpy and her black eyeliner slightly askew, but the thing that took my breath away was Debbie's thick luscious lips. After residing with over a dozen foster sisters I had never seen lips like Debbie's before. And I had to inspect those babies. It was only when I bent closer did I notice how pronounced they were and how they had a different aroma—a far more sweeter smell surrounded them. After taking in a lungful, to my excitement I discovered Debbie was wearing strawberry lip gloss. *"Oh yeah!"* I said to myself. Here I was inches away from a girl who was wearing strawberry gloss. And by the look of those lips, Debbie must have applied the gloss and let it dry before adding another application and another and another and another. I was so excited that my left leg began to jiggle.

The big moment. A life-altering experience. Who knows

where this could lead—holding hands, going steady, marriage? Kids? A home? And by the size of Debbie's house, her parents must be rich! My mind began to spin with ideas. I could . . . live in Duinsmoore, with this beautiful girl, in an incredible home with a garage, and I could build things like Dan does, and have Paul and David over when they came home after work. . . . I so can't believe my luck. All my problems, all my insecurities, all my worries would be solved with this one kiss. Not some peck on the cheek or someone who was "dared," but the real deal. Someone who wanted me. It was just a scene from one of those romance movies I had seen endless times. The only thing missing was violins in the background. My heart sped so fast that I thought it would burst through my chest. I carefully leaned forward trying to match Debbie's movements. For a moment I feared I'd miss those strawberry lips and plant one on Debbie's forehead, or if she suddenly straightened her back she'd think I was some pervert if I ended up kissing her on the upper part of her chest. Fighting off my nervousness, I tried to play it cool by slowly breathing in through my nose. But when I came within inches of meeting Debbie's lips, I kept my eyes wide open . . . for I didn't want to miss any of this.

The closer I came to making contact, I suddenly felt as if I were some astronaut on an Apollo mission to the moon with a commentator providing a progress report. *"Four feet . . . three feet . . . slight yaw to the right. Approaching two feet. Slow your rate of capture. Twelve inches. . . . Warning, warning, warning, close proximity alert, close proximity alert!*

Slow down breathing. Engage manual override. Ten inches. Eight. Stabilize forward motion. Wet lips. Prepare for contact. Six inches. Five . . . four . . . three . . . two—"

"Just what in the hell is going on here?" someone suddenly screeched, bringing me back to earth. *"Uh-oh,"* I warned myself, *"Houston, we have a problem."* As my upper torso lurched upward, instead of staring at Debbie's face or the deep crevices of her brightly striped blouse, I was now staring at a thick long fingernail pointing at me as if it were the barrel of Inspector Callahan's .44 Magnum. "It's you!" the woman bellowed.

"Me?" I blinked.

"Yes, you!" the woman reinstated.

"Me?" I asked.

"Don't go there with your cute little condescending tone. Not with me! You're that little . . . that little *F-child*, aren't you?" she sneered. All I could do was think that the second before The Eagle landed on moonbase Debbie, her mother must have seen what was about to happen and shoved her aside. "Answer me!" she demanded. "You're him!" she emphasized with another jab of her loaded Cruella De Vil fingernail. With the tingling excitement now gone, I braced myself for another serious scolding. "I know all about you and those, those, those foster people of yours; making all that money from the state to take in the likes of you. Who do you think you are? And how in the world did 'the association' ever approve of *your kind* to reside in *our* neighborhood? I know all about *your kind*. I'm informed. I'll have you know, I watch *60 Minutes.*

"You, young man, are nothing more than a filthy little hooligan! Just look at yourself: You reek of street trash. We don't allow trailer trash in *this* community! I don't know what you children do to become ... *foster children!*" The lady stuttered as she suddenly covered her mouth as if the words "foster children" were a one-way ticket to Hades. "Tell me, what was it you *did*, hmmm?

"Don't you even think of approaching my daughter or any of my children. My husband ... he has a gun and he's not afraid to pepper your backside with buckshot!" As if collecting herself, Debbie's mother lowered her voice as she bent forward. "Let me give you a piece of advice: Don't waste your time. *You* don't stand a chance. You don't have what it takes to make it. Believe me, I know. I went to college. I've seen it all." Pausing before giving me a sly crocodile smile, the "Brady Bunch" mother from hell then tossed her hair to one side, closing with, "I've been around and I've seen it all, so it's better for *you* that you're told now. Don't even bother. Stick with your own kind. You'll never be good enough!"

Before I could blink I could feel the force of the front door slam in my face. All I could do was stand by the door, digesting all that had just taken place. With every angry word Debbie's mom lashed out at me, I could feel myself shrinking to the size of an ant, until I was nonexistent.

"Dude, what a bummer!" David broke in. "What'd you do next?"

My mouth tightened as I confessed, "I ran past Paul on my way home, locked myself in my room, and cried."

"No way!" David howled. "You cried?"

"Yeah, like a baby. I heard shit like that all my life, but even so, I can't tell you how devastating it still made me feel."

"Did you ever see Debbie again?"

"Yeah," I sighed, "I saw her at the bus stop a few days later and I tried to say hi and make her laugh, but she acted as if I wasn't even there. Like I was invisible or something. One moment she likes me enough for a kiss and another I'm a leper. I don't get it, man. I'll never understand. I ain't ever gonna get married. No way. It's not worth it."

"That's right, brother," David nodded in approval. "No girls, no guns, and no drugs. Girls ain't nothin' but trouble! Who needs 'em, anyway?"

"That's right," I laughed. "Now, give me that *How to Pick up Girls* book. I have so got to practice."

8

⚬ഐ⚬

A Boy and His Car

I should have known. On a sunny Friday afternoon, on the last day of school of my sophomore year, June 1978, as I turned the corner to retrieve my recently purchased motorcycle, I shouldn't have been surprised to discover that it was stolen. I had a fair idea who did it, but at the moment it didn't matter. My ancient three-cylinder Kawasaki motorcycle was not some teenage status symbol, as much as it was a mode of transportation that enabled me to work full time at the local plastics factory. To add to my anxiety, I was due for work in less than three hours. Being seventeen and a half years old, I felt I was too old to ride my rusted ten-speed bike back and forth to work, especially when I had spent a fair amount of my savings buying and fixing up my Kawasaki. I was streetwise enough that I should have known better.

During the eight-mile walk home, streams of cars and trucks zoomed past me—some of which were filled with kids from school who honked their horns as they were driving home or to their summertime retreats—and only in-tensified my anger and jealousy. By the time I cut through a used car lot, I was so furious that I decided to buy one. I didn't think. I didn't analyze. I just knew I needed trans-portation. And I thought I was *grown up enough* to make the decision without the approval or advice of my foster parents.

I fully knew I was being taken advantage of by the car salesman with a smooth-talking pitch, an oily pompadour, a baby-blue polyester suit and white vinyl shoes, but yet I didn't care. I was about to empty over half of my savings for the down payment and make payments of $132 a month for thirty-six months on a car that was nearly six years old and had almost one hundred thousand miles on it. Having worked for a small independent defunct car dealership, washing cars, and being the all-around gofer, I learned the give-and-take of the purchasing transaction, but my stub-bornness refused to recede. I just didn't have the time to dicker. I needed a car that would get me to and from work or any other place I decided to explore. And with a car, in-stead of my motorcycle, I no longer had to be scared to death every time it rained or whenever the fog became so thick I couldn't see through the visor of my helmet. I would no longer have to endure near-frostbite conditions when I rode home from work in the middle of the night, or be terri-fied of someone not paying attention and turning into my lane while I was still in it. My biggest fear was hitting a spot of oil and wiping out at full speed and, with my luck, having someone run over me. A car would make my concerns a thing of the past, as well put me a major step closer to the independence of adulthood.

Less than an hour later, with a crumpled signed contract stuffed in my back pocket and a wide smile from the gold-toothed salesman, I eased from the car lot, taking an immediate left at the next block before carefully parking my car in front of the Turnboughs' home. My first ride lasted less than two minutes and a distance of under a thousand feet. I just didn't have time for joyriding. I ran through the empty house, peeled off my school clothes, threw on my work clothes, and frantically scrawled a note that I placed on the refrigerator door: *Someone stole my motorcycle, so I bought a car. Don't worry, I'll be safe. I know what I'm doing. I've given it serious thought. I got it all planned out. It's okay. See you later after work. Love, Dave.* Fearing the Turnboughs' imminent return—in which they would surely force me to sit down and explain my actions, possibly causing me to be late for work, or worse, return the car—I sprinted outside, eased into my prized Chevy Chevelle, and officially took my first drive.

The next Saturday morning, when I came home from the plastics factory after pulling a twelve-hour shift, Alice and Harold Turnbough gave a short "you're almost eighteen so we can't stop you from doing everything, and we only hope you know what you're getting into" speech. Part of me thought they would really lay into me. I was surprised and relieved that they did not browbeat me, yet, at the same time, a little scared that they knew something I didn't—as if they were passing on some coded message only maturity could decipher; like some gigantic shoe would fall from the heavens, squashing me, my car, and anything else I did without the Turnboughs' approval or protection. I only hoped I had not bitten off more responsibility than I could chew.

Exhausted as I was from the whirlwind of the last twenty-four hours, nothing could stop me from grabbing my cleaning supplies and marching outside. I was going to wash *my car*. Seven hours later, the Chevy looked better than new. I washed the exterior twice before applying two coats of Turtle Wax. The once faded blue vinyl roof now gleamed from five thick applications of Nu-Vinyl restorer. I vacuumed the inside, brushing and scouring every inch with a wet rag; and to get into the slots of the dust-filled heating vents, I used a toothbrush and a wet Q-tip. Only when the interior was soil and dust free, did I then apply the miracle shiner Armour-All on everything—the door handles, the scuffed parking brake, the inside roof, and the steering wheel. The final touch was resetting my scratchy AM radio stations. After taking a long shower, donning my best long-sleeved shirt, and downing a quick glass of orange juice, I triumphantly stepped outside to gaze at my accomplishment. I had a car. It was clean and it was all mine.

Starting the car, I let it idle for a minute as I inhaled my pine-scented air freshener. I then rolled down my window and eased my car down the block as slowly as possible, to provide everyone the opportunity of a proper gaze. Dave Pelzer had a set of wheels.

Informing the Turnboughs through another note, I was ready for my first journey: I was heading to Duinsmoore.

The drive south on the Bay Area's Highway 101 was sheer terror. My only experience driving had been driver's ed at school and it was months ago when I took the actual test. This was my first time driving for more than five minutes, let alone piloting a vehicle by myself. I stayed in the far right-hand lane, traveling at thirty-five miles per hour until I felt I had mastered the art of automotive control, a mere ten miles later. With all the confidence of a complete idiot, I drastically swung the Chevelle to the left, straddling two lanes at the same time. Once my heartbeat slowed, I kept a death grip on the steering wheel, surprisingly maintaining the speed limit, while trying not to kill anyone in the process. Having slid side to side in the newly shined bench seat, I made a mental note to go a little easy on the Armour-All cleaner next time. As the miles zoomed past, I began to relax. The radio helped dramatically as Joe Walsh screeched his comical, haphazard lifestyle song, "Life's Been Good To Me So Far."

As I carefully and slowly drove onto Duinsmoore Way before parking the car on the sidewalk in front of Michael Marsh's house, every head snapped in my direction. With the window rolled down I didn't pay any mind when one of the adults shrieked, "Oh my gawd, he has a car!" for I had arrived. With the Chevelle parked and brake set, I felt as if I were an exhausted pilot who had just flown nonstop across the Atlantic Ocean. I sat still as my brain ran through my self-imposed shutdown sequence. Getting out of the car, I met Paul and David, who had rushed over to inspect my prize. Remembering the line I had used when they had first seen my minibike, and with my arms folded across my chest, I leaned against the front end of the car and uttered, "Pretty cool, eh?"

Paul instantly rattled off a string of inquires. "Does it have a V-8?"

"No, straight six," I fired back, matching his tone.

"Exhaust headers?"

"No."

"Power steering?"

"Yep," I said, nodding my head.

"Power brakes?"

"No."

"FM radio? Eight-track tape player?"

"Only AM. It has an automatic transmission, a spare tire, a set of emergency roadside flares, the tires are almost new, and it's all mine," I proudly stated.

"Cool," David smiled as he rubbed his hands together, "road flares. We could do a lot of damage with those."

I raised a finger cutting David off. "Don't even think about it. A car is not a toy. This isn't a minibike, and those days of . . . of reckless abandonment are over," I preached with self-assurance.

"Now this," The Sarge began as he strolled over with a can of Coors clutched in his talons, "this is a crisis of sheer magnitude, far more deeper, far more sinister than Watergate." Lowering his sunglasses The Sarge continued to tease, "Tell me this 'Detroit Gas Guzzler' belongs to one of your orphan foster youth's cousin's next-door neighbor's foreign exchange student's friend. Tell me you're out joyriding. Tell me anything. Just don't tell me it's yours, my coordinately-challenged friend."

With a wide smile and a wave of my hand I confessed, "It most certainly is. Lock, stock, and a quart of motor oil."

The Sarge then raised his glasses to cover his eyes before uttering, "If I were chancellor of the Golden State, I would tar and feather the swine who graded you competent to obtain a license. God help us all."

Dan's only concern was, "You know this is a major responsibility." I nodded in agreement. Opening the hood before checking for any leaks under the car, Mr. Brazell gave me his approval. Rubbing his hand against the body, Dan smiled. "You had the car detailed?"

"No, sir," I boasted, "did the entire car myself. Came home from workin' a long shift, washed and waxed the car, and took a quick shower so I could make the drive down to see you," I proudly said to my mentor.

"All right," Dan laughed as he gave me a pat on the back, "just next time get some sleep before you slide behind the wheel, okay?" Over the next hour with just Dan and me in his garage, he went over in various details the dos and don'ts about driving and the standard in which he expected me to take care of the vehicle. Although I had heard the similar lectures about safety and the rules of the road from my instructor at driver's ed and from Mr. Turnbough, Dan's sincerity and indispensable knowledge of automobiles made me absorb everything all the more. As Mr. Brazell went into detail about simple but technical aspects of vehicle maintenance, I suddenly realized it was the first time

Dan and I were alone and how he addressed me more as an adult rather than some annoying chaotic child, as he did when we first met. Walking away from Dan, I felt as if I had just attended a semester of college.

"So, did my dad give you the big lecture bit?" Paul jabbed as he raised he eyebrows.

Opening the hood of my car so I could look and remember the different aspects of the engine before I forgot, I replied to Paul, "No, he was pretty cool. I wish I was his apprentice so I could learn more from him. There's much more to a car than just driving it."

"He's not a god!" Paul bellowed.

I gently closed the enormous hood, nodded at Paul, and kept my mouth shut. Over the last few visits whenever David or I said anything about Mr. Brazell, especially if we praised him, Paul would sometimes seem to tense up or shoot off like a rocket. Having lived my early childhood with a father that wasn't there for my brothers or me, and then living in so many foster homes, I could sense the real thing when I saw it. To me Dan was not only around the same age as my biological father, but, more important, lived by a set of values I greatly admired. Mr. Brazell was everything I had so desperately craved my father to be.

With Mr. Brazell's words still ringing in my ears and wanting to act more like an adult, I laid down my very own rules; how others were to behave if they wanted to ride with me. "Now listen up," I announced in a deep voice. "There is to be no goofing around when we're in the car, none whatsoever. Everyone wears a seat belt. No yelling, no distractions of any kind."

I found myself running out of steam when David laughed. "Dude, *you* can't be serious, man! . . . You're the Pelz!"

"Not anymore," I quickly countered, trying to act more than my age. "A car is not a toy. No drinking, no eating, no swearing in the car, and if we go cruising . . . you two should help pitch in with the gas."

"We gotta *pay* to ride with you?!" Paul shouted. "Who turned you into a cheapskate?"

"Do you have any idea what it costs in gas, oil, car insurance, and the amount of maintenance to keep a car in pristine condition, hmm? The tires alone . . ." I stopped midsentence as I discovered myself regurgitating the same "it takes a lot to keep a car running" speech that my foster father had given me before and Paul's father just moments ago. Part of me wanted nothing more than for the three of us to race off with the windows rolled down, music blaring, and just ride, but yet with all the time I had spent on my car and all the lectures, coupled with my lack of experience behind the wheel, I wanted to take things as slowly and carefully as possible.

After Paul and David received permission from their parents, the three of us idled our way down the block. Miles later I continued to keep the car ten miles below the speed limit, until we pulled over to a run down Foster Freeze hamburger stand. "Man," Paul whined, "you drive worse than my mother."

"If The Sarge were here he'd say 'this is a sad state of

affairs,' " Howard commented. "Come on, it's Saturday! We got a car! We're young! We're bulletproof! And you're driving like Pa Kettle from the Ozarks!"

"Have you two ever seen *The Highway of Death*?" I retaliated between sips of my soda. My naive friends didn't respond. "I didn't think so. Once you see that film . . ."

"Wait a minute," David exclaimed, "is that the film where they stage those car crashes that make you throw up so you won't drink and drive? And all the while they have that guy who preaches in a low voice about 'driving takes responsibility, be a responsible driver, drive responsibly'?" David emphasized using his fingers for quotations. "Man, I hear that film is so cool. Did anybody lose it in your class?"

Shaking his head, Paul informed David in detail that the film used fake blood, mannequins, and parts of dead animals for the more dramatic scenes.

Losing grip on my "mature" act, I lowered my defenses and returned to my old Duinsmoore ways and announced, "Heed my words, young squires: Once you endure *The Highway of Death*, your life will forever be transformed. *Now*, let's see what this baby can do!" The three of us looked at each other and slapped our hands together, slamming the huge metal doors behind us. As I drove the car by my old high school, I found myself more relaxed and confident than I had been just a few minutes ago. The overwhelming pressure of *worrying* about responsible driving gave way to the moment of just being with Paul and David.

As the three of us slowly cruised through the streets, glancing at the beautiful estates, we became lost, ending up at the end of a dirt road. Careful not to dirty the car, I cautiously tried to back up, but the car refused to move. So I tried shifting the car in forward gear. As I carefully applied more pressure to the gas pedal, nothing seemed to happen. Frustrated and embarrassed in front of my friends, I mashed down on the accelerator. The engine roared to life. The Chevelle kicked up a wave of loose dirt as the car bolted away. The sensation was like piloting a rocket plane. When we finally reached the entrance to the paved street, I skidded the car to a stop, then stared at the cloud of dust behind. From the backseat, David leaned over to pat me on the back. "Cool man, did you mean to do that?"

"Why, of course," I responded

"Can you do it again?" David pleaded.

"I could, but . . ." I hesitated.

"He didn't mean to spin out that way. And I say he can't do it again. No way!" Paul challenged.

I turned away from Paul and stared out the windshield. As much as I fought it, I was about to break a long list of my own set of cardinal rules, which above all included my rigid standard of keeping the car from the slightest speck of dirt or debris. But the surge of excitement and sheer power I felt from my fingers being wrapped around the wheel was beyond anything I had ever experienced. "All right, roll up your windows and strap in tight, boys. We're goin' for a ride," I advised a second before I floored the accelerator. For a moment the three of us felt a slight shudder as a stream of dirt and loose rock kicked up from behind the car. I barely eased off the gas pedal when the car shot forward. As the Chevy quickly picked up speed, the end of the road suddenly filled the front windshield. It was then I became unsure of my driving capabilities. As I drifted slightly to the right while easing off the accelerator, Paul and David declared their fear of an imminent crash.

"This isn't funny! Slow down, slow down!" Paul shouted beside me, while David broke out in laughter. When the last mailbox whizzed by, I took my foot off the accelerator, counted to one, and simultaneously stomped on the brake pedal as I swung the car wildly to the left.

Stealing a glance from the rearview mirror, I could see David's body slide over from the inertia. In the midst of everything, I made yet another mental note about reducing my next Armour-All application.

Recalling a technique—do not overcorrect in a skid— that I had learned from driver's ed, I let go of the steering wheel for a split second, let it spin freely in front of me, then grabbed it again with my fumbling fingers. When I felt the back end of the car swing to the left, I again punched the gas pedal, which propelled the car in the opposite direction of where we just came.

Even though I had visualized everything in my mind and had salivated with glee whenever I had seen the same stunt performed with complete ease in hundreds of action films, what my excited passengers didn't know, what they failed to realize when seeing my clenched teeth, was that I was consumed with terror. Not for driving down a dirt road at breakneck speed, nor turning my car in a teapot-

sized space, but that I was now in the middle of a thick
brown dust storm that I had just created, and I hadn't the
vaguest clue of where I was heading. And as if I didn't
have enough anxiety to keep my pulse racing, the back end
of the heavy Chevelle kept swaying from side to side, forcing me to counter the oscillation by counter-correcting the
steering wheel, which I discovered only amplified the problem. By sheer luck, to the left of my window I caught a
glimpse of another mailbox streak past. It was only then that
I felt I was indeed heading in the right direction. Unless, of
course, with my luck, I had overcorrected and swung the
vehicle a full 360 degrees. Either way, in a matter of seconds
the three of us would indeed test the fate of the gods to find
out how truly bulletproof we were. When I saw beams of
bright filtered light like rays from heaven above ahead of
me, I eased off the accelerator and brought the car to a stop
at the entrance to the street.

When I casually opened my door and stepped out, I
knew Paul and David would rip into me. Maybe, I thought,
I could get away with telling them I had *planned* on scaring
them straight all along; like some sick, perverted, twisted,
Highway of Death real-life experience. For a few minutes the
three of us stared in awe at the billows of dirt that refused
to settle. I braced myself as Paul leaned forward and jabbed
a finger in my face. *"That ..."* he roared, *"... was the
coolest thing ever!"*

"Totally!" David echoed. "Just like in the movies!"

"Where'd you learn to do that?" Paul asked.

"Well," I replied, leaning on the side of the car as I continued to look at the street, "if you must know, it's the Steve McQueen movie *Bullitt* meets *The French Connection* . . . with just a touch of driver's ed."

After hosing off the dust from the car at a nearby car wash, and after a series of "cross our hearts and hope to die" promises, we decided to keep our latest exploit to ourselves, and I slowly eased the Chevelle back into Duinsmoore. With a wide smile glued on my face I must have been extremely confident of our covert activity, until Dan nonchalantly strolled over, bent down, and removed several pieces of a bush from under the rear bumper.

Huddling together a distance away from Mr. Brazell's garage, in whispered tones we replayed our adventure and planned new ones. Not only could we use the car as a sure-fire, pick-up-chicks and take-us-anywhere mobile, but it was now a chance to do stuff we had only seen on the big screen.

Later that evening with the car windows rolled down, the three of us made our inaugural cruise down California's renowned El Camino Real—The Strip. The famed highway basically ran from the Bay Area and down past south Los Angeles. For years I had overheard about all the action—daring drag races at the stoplights, wild parties and tricked-out cars, and those wide-eyed girls who would do practically anything with any guy who just had a set of wheels. *Now* the three of us stood a chance with the opposite sex. Just days before, those stuck-up Farah Fawcett look-alikes wouldn't give me the time of day, *but now I had a car*. A car that I hadn't borrowed from my well-to-do parents, or a set of wheels some relative gave me as a present for my sixteenth birthday, but a car that I worked for, a car that belonged to me. And this car would surely prove to any foxy lady that I was definitely a guy worth her time and, possibly, her unbridled desires. Sitting tall in the driver's seat and with the speed of a snail I drove David and Paul and joined the hundreds of cars that deliberately crawled from stoplight to stoplight. The only difference: While the souped-up cars raced their engines, I proudly blared my AM radio to the easy-listening station playing nonstop Barry Manilow songs.

Yet, after several loops on the famed strip within the confines of Menlo Park, the only attention we received were taunts from either the older, extreme-looking teens with their white T-shirts and black leather jackets, or the preppie kids with perfectly combed hair and sharp clothes who howled with laughter at us. The same girls who would usually slither on car hoods while showing off their eight-inch wooden platform shoes, black hip-hugger cut-off pants, and tight stretchy fluorescent tube-tops that seemed to reveal everything in the cool night air only offered us a middle finger thrust high into the air or buried in their throats, acting as if the three of us were so revolting they would throw up. But the highlight of our cruise down El Camino Real came unexpectedly at a stoplight when a compact car brimming with excited girls lurched to a sudden stop. Smiling at us, two of them seemed to become frantic as they screeched, "Oh, baby, baby! Take me, take me now!" as the three of us stared at one another with wide eyes and strands of dribble seeping from the sides of our mouths. A moment later the girls' car rocketed away while they laughed aloud. Feeling humiliated, Paul, David, and I decided to call it a night. Besides, it was getting late. By the time I parked the car in Mr. Marsh's driveway it was almost nine-thirty.

The next morning the three of us regaled in our adventure on The Strip. None of us seemed to realize reliving the event was more entertaining than actually being there. Then in the late afternoon, after hours of replaying every detail, Paul, David, and I became excited imagining how much more fun, how cool we would become, and how "lucky" we would get the *next* time we cruised El Camino Real.

But our adventures on four wheels were short-lived. In less than two months after buying the car, I suddenly became laid off from the plastics factory. As my luck went, when the loan officer from the car dealership discovered I was unemployed, and even after I proved I had enough money in my savings account to make payments for more than a year, I was forced to return my beloved Chevy. Within days, out of the blue, Mike Marsh phoned me at my foster parents' home, informing me he would cosign the car loan. After hanging up the phone, I wasn't sure how to feel. The more the car wasn't mine, the more I craved it. But yet I knew how much Mike and his caring wife, Sandy, busted their butts working every day. During weekdays, as Mike returned home from work, he'd honk his horn the moment he turned into Duinsmoore. A second later, with Sandy perched in her ancient oxidized-blue VW van, she'd back out of the driveway ready to work a twelve-hour shift at the local hospital.

Over the years since I had first met the Marshes, the entire household adopted me like some quasi-nephew. They rarely turned me down for a place to stay when I visited Paul and Dave. But even when times were tough for them, I always had a seat at their table. That Friday afternoon, as Mr. Marsh and I waited at the loan office at the car dealership, I turned to confess for the millionth time my sincere appreciation. When he nodded back at me, I caught a look in his eyes. It was then I realized just how far the Marshes were sticking their necks out to help me. Suddenly I felt like a bloodsucker. As much as I thought I needed the car to search for a better job—anything other than the bewildering fast-food joints—and as much as I had seemingly become emotionally attached to that particular car, I suddenly felt slimy about the entire situation. In unison, the "Doc Savage" of Duinsmoore and his trusty young ward stood up and departed the dealership.

On the solemn drive to Duinsmoore Way, without thinking, I blurted out to Mike, "You would have signed for the loan. I mean, even though there's a chance I could screw up and miss a payment, putting you and Sandy in a bind, you would have done it for me. I don't get it. I mean, you *really* don't know me," I stated, realizing he didn't know all of my past. "You're constantly berating me and the guys because 'we're an aimlessly roaming herd of mindless bison,' but yet you trust me. I just don't get it."

"I can read you," Mike stated matter-of-factly. I looked up, shaking my head.

"I've learned a lot from 'Nam. A lot about myself. One thing is in the heat of battle, and I'm talkin' about a really serious firefight when lives are on the line—and I don't mean any of that dramatic Hollywood crapola you see on the big screen, but the real deal—you find out what you're made of. I'm not talkin' about killing someone. Any backwoods hillbilly idiot can do that. But living with it afterward, that's the thing. Living with yourself after all the disgusting disturbing shit you've done just to make it out alive, that's what I'm preaching. Or being there, to back your brothers in arms when all this bad crap is going on around you, that's what I'm getting at.

"It's kinda like this, my young apprentice: You're on the cusp and your mind is a sponge absorbing everything around you. So absorb this: There's a lot of folks that talk a big game. A lot of them just talk out the side of their mouths. I can back it up. Not with guns, explosives, or some James Bond kung fu moves, but here," Mike emphasized, tapping the side of his head with his finger. "It's all in the head. That's it, plain and simple. All your troubles, all your woes are between your ears.

"Then, there are those who suddenly face a situation, a predicament they can't snap their fingers and have it instantly taken care of. They lock up, they freeze, 'cause they've never experienced anything like that before—like at 'Nam in the bush, in the middle of a firefight, and some of them can last for hours or even days. In my former career as a ranger, if you don't pull your load, or if you lock up, or if you're having a bad day out there, you can get someone killed. Then, there are the Jimmy Olsons—the do-gooder types from cornfed heartland USA, the skinny, moppy-head teen that never had a date, got egged at the high school prom; the kid that simply takes a lot of shit 'cause that's what life gave 'em—those are the kinda folks who will do whatever it takes to get things done. I've seen it thousands of times in 'Nam; they don't bitch, they just do! They'll walk in a minefield to rescue a member of a squad. They jump in the middle of a firefight to carry off a wounded guy on their shoulders, the same jerk who gave the Jimmy Olson kid a truckload of crud a few days ago. And Jimmy Boy carries that lump of shit up a hill, through a forest, with bullets whizzing past them in full gear because that's the type of guy he is. Not for fame, fortune, chicks, or a can of Coors.

"There are those who just do 'cause they've endured a lot already and try to make things better for others. *Capisce*, amigo?" Turning to me as he took off his sunglasses to emphasize his point, Mike conceded, "You know, David, one doesn't have to go off to some foreign country armed with guns and grenades to fight and overcome one's war."

The statement hung inside the tiny Toyota as Mike weaved his way through the rush hour traffic. I wasn't sure how to react, as I didn't know if he knew how close he was to unlocking my own private hell. I swallowed hard and turned to stare at the passing cars. "Hey man, don't sweat it," The Sarge joked as he tapped me on the shoulder. "I'm just talkin' trash. I know I get a bit long-winded, and half the time I'm full of it, but I know you and I would have signed the paperwork and not looked back. Mr. Pelzer, you're okay in my book. Keep your chin up, and your eyes wide open. Tomorrow's prince was yesterday's frog. That's not the only car in town—there's a lot of Detroit metal on the road these days and tomorrow is another day."

"Thanks, Mike," I smiled.

"No sweat-de-da, Jimmy Olson. No sweat," Mike chanted.

Whatever disappointment I might have felt for myself about the sudden loss of mobile independence dissipated by the time Mike and I arrived at Duinsmoore. When I confessed to David and Paul what had happened, they simply raised their shoulders as if it were no big deal. Then instead of blindly heading off at high speeds in search of unknown adventure, David and I now leisurely strolled around the block. If anything, I joked, the lack of wheels limited our chances of doing anything too stupid.

Stopping in front of my old foster home, where the Welshes had moved out some time ago, David said that a family from Italy had moved in and the father was an engineer who worked with NASA on the upcoming Space Shuttle Transport-Orbiter at nearby Moffet Field. In awe of meeting a real scientist, I instantly bombarded him with questions. How do astronauts go to the bathroom in space?

Does the lack of gravity have any effect on how blood pumps into the heart? Or reduce the growth of hair? The engineer simply smiled at me, as he patted me on the head as if I were a dog, while answering, "Yes, yes, yes," over and over again. It wasn't until David and I came to Paul's house that David informed me the Italian scientist understood very little English.

"But not to worry," David smiled, "The Sarge has been dubbed the 'Ambassador of Goodwill' and has already taught him the meaning of Coors beer!"

Howard's comment eased the tension I felt inside of knowing that once again I became overly nervous and had gotten ahead of myself by babbling in front of the NASA scientist. By the time I was eight years old I knew I wanted to either fly jets or become a volcanologist. To me volcanoes symbolized the creation of the world, but also held an alluring, yet incredibly destructive force as well. Meeting a real scientist that dealt with cutting-edge space products was not only cool, but suddenly made me contemplate my own future desires. It also made me realize that I had pushed aside a deep aspiration that seemed so attainable and important to me as a young child. For years I had always driven myself to survive, rather than focusing on what I wanted to do with my life. Meeting the NASA engineer made me think of things I had long since forgotten.

"Hey, Pelz," David interrupted, "if you want to see something cool, you should check this out." Moments later I stood in absolute awe of Paul's re-creation: an exact copy of the *Star Wars* R2D2. As Paul rattled off the challenges he overcame, I learned the replica was built without a single diagram and only what Paul kept in his head. Kneeling down, examining Paul's droid, it seemed perfect—from the revolving head to the exact blue squares.

Praising Paul, all I could utter was, "I can't believe it!"

Paul knelt down to adjust the droid's eye. "If I had some servos and a remote control, I could make it move like the real thing."

"Don't sell yourself short, pal," I praised. "In a word: It's incredible."

Paul simply nodded, brushing off the compliment as he fiddled with his creation. Later, as David and I walked off, all I could think to say was that Paul was an absolute genius.

"Yep, I know," David echoed, "that he is. You wanna know how he did it?" I shook my head yes. "He disappears for about three weeks. I mean, after school he's gone, invisible. Come to find out he's at the movies. He must have seen *Star Wars* forty maybe fifty times. Then he basically locks himself in his room making notes, then he's in Dan's garage building the thing. He didn't tell a soul. Is that cool or what? And hey, get this: The NASA guy, Franco, he checks out Paul's work, and I mean he measured it from head to toe as if using some micrometer, and tells everyone, and I mean everyone, that Paul has what it takes to work for NASA! Franco says the NASA folks are always scouting for brainiacs like Paul. The younger they find 'em, the better."

"No way!" I shouted. "Paul at NASA? Awesome!"

"The guy's a bit moody and a total loner at times and I

always knew he was smart, but man, I'm an idiot compared to him," David commented. "Last week I was at Mr. Brazell's garage and just hangin' out when some of the guys were talking about Paul's future with Houston or even Cape Canaveral."

"But what about you?" I inquired. "What do you see yourself doing?"

"I like building things. I may go into construction, maybe carpentry, or a plumber."

"And what's the consensus from 'The Think Tank'?" I joked.

"Yeah, they see me in that line of work. I helped Dan out a bit and he says I have good hands. But you . . ." David added.

My eyes grew wide as I imagined the group of men huddled close together, conspiring against me for all the chaos I caused. "What'd they say?"

"Well," David admitted, "the odds are five to one that you're gonna end up in jail or become a street sweeper."

"Five to one? That sucks. So, who bet against me?" I pleaded.

Using his fingers to count the votes, David began with, "Um, Mr. Neyland for one, obviously. Mr. Jolly, Mr. Ballow for what reason I don't know, but I do know he doesn't like you. Anyway, Dan's in your favor but The Sarge and I abstained."

"Abstained? What the hell are you guys, the Soviet Union?" I fired back. "Why didn't you two stand up for me, man?"

"Yo, Pelz, it's just a joke. Take a chill pill. But seriously, what do you see yourself doing, you know, with the rest of your life?"

Stunned, I stood in front of my friend with my mouth hung open. "I . . . I don't know."

After a lapse of embarrassing silence, David said, "I sure do miss that car of yours."

Feeling like a little kid that was grounded without his bicycle, I asked, "So, what do you wanna do this weekend?"

"Oh, man, I forgot to tell you. I gotta job. I work part time at the hardware store. I'm gonna be late, I gotta run."

"A job? No way," I shouted. "What for?"

"Duh, so I can get a car. Anyway, I gotta go. You'll have to hang out with Paul this weekend. Catch ya later." Howard rushed before sprinting off to his house. Before I could yell at him that Paul would probably spend the entire weekend locked in his room, David was out of sight.

I stood in the middle of the street dumbstruck. When I turned away from the Howards' house, I realized how still the neighborhood was. There wasn't a kid in sight, and all I could hear was my own breathing. For some reason I felt scared. My only friends in the entire world and I were growing in different directions. And, for the first time since discovering Duinsmoore Way, I found myself completely alone.

9

Wake-Up Call

It was July of 1978. I woke up before sunrise, suddenly realizing in less than six months I would become a legal adult. David Howard's off-the-cuff remark just days ago, of what I wanted to do with my life suddenly paralyzed all other thoughts. As I lay in bed listening to my own breathing, I now felt as though I had run out of time. Even though I had two more years of high school left—not only because I had been held back in the first grade but because I was born late in the calendar year—if I were to remain in school I would have to do so on my own support. For some stupid reason I had kept telling myself that as long as I stayed in school, I was somehow protected from stepping out into the void of a vast world. As much as I was excited about being my own person, I had always seemed safe since becoming an adult was so far off. But I was much older now.

At least, I told myself, I still had a fair amount of savings. But the short time I had the Chevy taught me that things unexpectedly can come up that can chip away at my financial safety net. I could only imagine what it would be like being "out there" when it truly mattered. I ridiculed myself that I was less than two hundred days shy of voting age now, riding from town to town searching for another job on a ratty temperamental ten-speed bicycle.

In part because I dreaded everything about high school, the sad fact that my grades hovered above dismal, and the painful fact that it was expensive, I never considered college. I had fantasized about enlisting in the U.S. Air Force and to eventually become a fireman like my father. But after taking the military entrance exam at school and failing miserably both times, I wasn't quite so sure. I also toyed with the idea of attending a technical school so I could work with sheet metal and possibly one day work side by side with Dan, but I felt I was too inept for any of the classes, especially when it came to measurements. Just a short time ago I had convinced myself I knew everything I would need to know to survive in the real world. Now my stupidity and arrogance was about to bite me in the behind.

My existence would be that of manual labor. Since I didn't have enough brains, I would survive by relying on my brawn—and a string-bean brawn at that. As long as I could come home to a nice, well-kept place that I could call my own, with a reliable clean car, and without ever worrying about where my next meal would come from, I would be content. But I simply no longer wanted to just get by from hustling my tail off for a few dollars, back and forth in the vast maze of fast-food chains. In my heart I knew there had to be something better out there for me. All I had to do was discover it and conquer it for myself.

Yet after pedaling as far as my bike could take me, the only professions that would consider me for employment were those in the quickie hamburger arena. Dejected, I scanned through the want ads, discovering opportunities for those who "craved a challenge, were highly motivated, willing to make untold sums of money, and receive their own automobile, free of charge, in the exciting field as . . . a car sales associate!" The last thing I wanted to do was wear tacky polyester suits and squeeze every dime from hardworking folks who simply wanted to own an automobile. But, then again, I began to convince myself, this job would solve two problems for me: First, I wouldn't have to break my back and come home covered in sweat and grime every day for the rest of my life and, second, I would have a car, and a new one at that. The next day I put on my best terry cloth shirt and casually brushed the white flakes from my shoulders before happily appearing for an interview for my new career.

As impressed as the sales managers may have been from my overpleasing, I-can-do-anything intensity, they felt I was a wee bit too young and inexperienced for their prestigious positions. Back at the Turnboughs' I brooded over my age, feeling trapped in the middle—not being old enough to work in the adult arena, yet tired of and overqualified for flipping burgers and cleaning bathrooms for the rest of my life. But the more car lots turned me away, the more I persisted. Luckily, after a few relentless weeks and dozens of interviews with other dealerships, I was hired by a Ford dealership on the conditions that my pay was based strictly on commission and I would not receive a car. I didn't care. I was just ecstatic to have a different kind of opportunity. Knowing this was a career that could possibly change my life, I immediately rushed out, cut my shoulder-length hair, and purchased a *full* wardrobe—two suits, two shirts, and three ties.

But after a few months of the high-pressure grind from furious managers who either hyped the sales staff every Friday morning at the weekly meetings, spinning fables of untold riches, or threatened us with doom and banishment, I quickly lost interest in the job. I hated competing with forty slimy salesmen who did practically anything— running to attack anybody that walked onto the car lot, or playing the psychological "if I could ... would you?" games with the customer—in their desperate attempts to get the poor soul to commit to buying a car *right then*.

I lasted four months. At that time it was the largest Ford dealership in the continental United States, but I still left, and I announced—of little surprise to Alice and Harold Turnbough—that I would not be returning to high school either. It seemed beyond me, after dressing in corduroy suits and mismatched frayed ties, working in a high-pressured fast-paced job during the summer, to simply come back to school wearing faded bell-bottom jeans and sit at a desk while trying to comprehend social science or the importance of Shakespeare, as the kids around me chewed bubble gum and gossiped within their cliques. I knew I was making a huge mistake, but after working and flourishing in an adult world that could pay more in a single day than two weeks of busting my hump, at my age and for all my social perplexities, I believed high school was a huge step backward for me.

Even though unemployed, I at least now proudly drove a rust-infested 1974 Chevy Vega that I owned outright. With the Vega, I finally learned not to strip every gear in the transmission, but now prayed that every time the car attempted to crawl up a hill the gas filter wouldn't clog up and stall the car in traffic; or whenever I took the car on the freeway that the ultra-sensitive clutch didn't suddenly break down, leaving me stranded as cars whizzed by.

The first time I triumphantly piloted the Vega to Duinsmoore, it mattered little to me that the car backfired every ten feet or so while leaving a trail of gray smoke. Even when Dan gave a quick inspection before turning away displeased, I still stood tall. But only after The Sarge blasted me that he had purchased a Vega when they were new and how he couldn't get rid of it fast enough did I begin to doubt the validity of my surprisingly good deal when I had dickered for the compact hatchback. "Well," Marsh shook his head, "at least at school you won't have to suffer any envy from your compadres."

Without thinking, I squinted up at Michael while shaking my head. "School? I haven't been to school in months. I dropped out!"

"Was that before or after someone dropped you on the head?" Marsh blasted.

I tried to calm him down, explaining my situation that I still had two years to complete while being out on my own. To me it didn't make sense to stay. "Besides," I surmised, "I got a career selling cars. I'm doing fine."

"Right," Marsh agreed with false praise. "You're nearly eighteen, unemployed, or excuse me, 'between jobs,' an academic flunky, driving around in an aluminum death trap. Yep . . . sounds like you're doing just fine. And tell me, young Rockefeller, what if you can't find placement in the grand odyssey of being a car huckster? What then, pray tell?"

I had expected this. The Turnboughs, having had dozens upon dozens of kids in my similar position, were slightly more understanding. But I knew that Mr. and Mrs. Marsh, as well as Dan, would blow their tops when I finally told them. It wasn't like the end of the world, for I already had another plan that I had discussed with Paul and David some time ago. "Well, if you must know," I slowly began to mumble in a low voice, suddenly feeling less confident, "I thought about going to Hollywood. . . ."

"As what?!" Mike interrupted. "The next prodigy discovery for George Lucas or Steven Spielberg? Oh, I get it, you want to take a chance at the leading man's roles, right? Trust me on this, Slim. Roger Moore is ensconced on *Her Majesty's Secret Service* and Clint Eastwood isn't going to 'high plain drift' out of town."

I kept my mouth shut until Mike ran out of steam. "No man, you don't get it. I'm not gonna be an actor. . . ."

"Thank God! For now I won't have to call Frank Sinatra

and tell him all the lovely damsels are about to flee his harem and flock to your tent. I'm sure ol' Blue Eyes will be most appreciative."

Losing control, I yelled, "I'm not going to Hollywood to become an actor! I'm gonna be a stuntman!"

Mike was speechless. For the first time since I had known him, The Sarge—The Great Communicator, who fought for truth, justice, and a six pack of Coors—was stunned stupid. The only sound evident was the raspy breathing that escaped his lungs. I also noticed that for the first time Mike had a set of thick veins that were now pulsating from his forehead.

"Let me get this straight," he began, "you lost your job at the plastics factory, which I say good riddance to. You had to return your Chevelle, due to lack of employment. So far, I understand. Then, you get a brainstorm that if you sell cars, the dealership will grant you a demo to drive around in, but, come to find out, for reasons of common sense and enormous liability, the good people at Ford Motor Company decided not to grant you this privilege. So, you purchase this . . . this jalopy"—The Sarge pointed at my humble Vega—"from some loser who was probably turned away from every low-life car lot from here to Baja, and who most likely tried to parlay this piece of excrement as a trade-in for another car. Tell me, young Skywalker, do you really think 'The Force' was with you on this good deal? When this guy sold you *this* car, did you sell him *another* car from that Ford establishment that you so proudly worked for?"

Since the transaction had happened so fast, I didn't have the chance to think it all through as deeply as Mike said. "Come to think of it, he never bought a car. But," I excitedly defended, "the guy does have my card and promised to give me a call."

"*The guy*, is that who he is, 'the guy'? You don't even know his name, do you?

"I apologize." He continued, "It appears I have deviated from my plethora of deductions. So, as of now, at this moment, you have four rubberlike tires, an AM radio, a shell of a car being held together with Band-Aids and bubble gum, and a mode of transport that will only get you ten feet in your journeys, and that's with you pushing from behind. You're a few hundred dollars shy in your token bank account. In turn, you drop out of high school to, 'to pursue a career in the exciting world of automotive sales' in which now you are unemployed, or *excu-u-u-u-se me*," Mike said in his Steve Martin voice, "as they say in Hollywood: You're simply on hiatus. And if all else fails you're gonna become a stuntman? Is that the gist of it? The only thing you haven't told me is that you might be a little bit pregnant."

"That's impossible," I said to the last statement, trying to keep Mike from blowing a gasket.

"Oh no, not for you it's not. You're like some strange amphibian, some frog from the darkest jungles of South America; one day you're male, then next you're a female carrying a bounty of eggs."

"Wow." I stood in front of Mike fascinated. "Are you for real? I didn't know that."

"You would if you went to school!" Mike fired back. "So tell me, stunt-wanna-be extraordinaire, how does a person of your stature and grace, who can't throw a baseball, can't catch a Frisbee, who has never played any sport in his entire life, with the aptitude and coordination of an invalid, accomplish such feats of grace, balance, precision, and courage, without getting turned into hamburger?"

I started to see where he was headed.

"What's your plan? Something of this importance must have been thought through. Do you even have a plan? Do you have any contacts?" Before I could inform Mike that I had indeed given the idea much thought of cashing out my bank account and hiding the large bills in my shoes, then praying the car would make it to Southern California, where I could get a job part time selling cars while taking classes *somewhere*, learning my new craft before working professionally on the big screen. I had figured four to six weeks, maybe half a year's time max before I'd be on my way to fame and fortune.

But The Sarge refused to back down. "I can see it now: As you pilot your dilapidated Vega, your trusty steed, as it may, through the Boulevard of Dreams, and the mayor of Hollywood, the Grand Pooh-Bah himself dressed in ceremonial garb, will stand on a podium addressing a throng of spectators, proclaiming *Dave Pelzer Day*, then hand you a key to the city. You're in like Flint, pal. You've got it made."

I rolled my eyes at his sarcasm. "I know what you're saying. And, I know it ain't gonna be like that. And I know I may not make it . . . but . . ."

Mike put a hand on my shoulder. "Trust me, Slim, I *know* I'm bombarding you more than the battle of Khe Sanh, which, by the way, was a seventy-seven-day siege in the Vietnam war, if you still have an interest in world history. I'm not tryin' to pee on your new set of boots, if you had any that is, but right now and I mean right at this moment in your life, as you make that step into adulthood, I cannot emphasize enough to you, because of your luck and everything else that swirls around your little solar system, all that's against you. Right now you have one foot in the grave and the other one on a banana peel. Out there in the world, it's a lot different than you think. Look at my bride and me; all we do is work our tailbones off. And that's every bloody day. You've only had a taste of it. Just wait till you get married and have a litter of your own. Everything's peachy keen, then one of your kids needs to see the dentist and you're losing sleep at night thinking how in the hell are you going to scrounge that extra $317 for fillings. It's a bitch to get ahead, let alone hold your own. And what if something happens to you, and it will— you fracture a bone, you're out of work, or with your luck you'd probably become paralyzed."

"But that ain't gonna happen to me," I countered.

"Slim, if I hear those words *ain't gonna*, one more time . . . You better choose some new words from your vernacular."

Squinting my eyes, I stuttered, "Ver-nac-u-lar?"

"Look it up in your dictionary. If you weren't an obtuse high school dropout, you'd know that word and a cornucopia of other things that would prepare you in the ways of the world. And *that's* precisely my point: You're way out of your league, Slim. If you don't have a basic education you won't amount to diddly. Ever! And that *ain't gonna happen* to me attitude doesn't fly. I admit that when I was your age I thought I was bulletproof. Everybody does. Did you know I used to be a mountain climber?"

"Wow!" I gasped.

"I'm not talking Mount Everest with Sir Hillary, but I'm here to tell ya, my overzealous, ignorant Sherpa, a lot of folks are so gung ho, thinking nothing's gonna happen to them and all they gotta do is put one foot in front of the other and watch where they step. That's an okay plan, but that's not enough. It's not making it to the summit that counts, but making it back down to base camp in one piece with all your fingers and toes. I'm here to tell ya, Adventure Boy, in the game of life shit happens. Up there, there's avalanches, windstorms so bad you can't see your hand in front of you. And something always, and I mean always, happens to a member of your team. Up there when, not if, but when the shit hits the fan, the higher you go, meaning the deeper you get into it, you can't get anybody down and they die. I'm not trying to be a drama queen here, but I'm trying to get through that thick noggin of yours that you're stumbling up a mountain, without any equipment or expertise and into a blizzard, but you're still at base camp. Am I getting through?"

I nodded my head.

Marsh's throbbing vein in his forehead began to recede. "I just don't see you as a replacement for someone like Burt

161

Reynolds who, by the way, played football in his youth and almost made it to the big leagues before a knee injury sidelined him. I even think he did a stint as a stuntman before making it to the big screen. And I surely don't see you schlepping cars for an eternity. You're at that fork in the road now, son. This is your time to think, really think about where you're at, what you're doing, and where you're going. You haven't passed the point of no return just yet. You've still got a few months, and if I were you I'd make 'em count."

Mr. Marsh was right. And so was Dan, who just a couple of weeks ago had driven over to my foster home to pick up my battered motorcycle that I had sold to Paul. Mr. Brazell sat in my bedroom for over an hour pleading with me to think carefully about my half-baked scheme. In reality it was a simple idiotic fantasy that Paul, David, and I fed into whenever I performed a stunt—driving down a street backward while staring straight ahead, which I had picked up from the Burt Reynolds movie *Hooper*, about the drama and endless adventures of a Hollywood stuntman. Thinking back, the idea began as a release from my mundane life— working twelve-hour workdays at the car dealership for weeks at a time, only to return home to collapse in my messy room. My sole relaxation was either sleep, watching movies, or my visits with Paul and David. Because I had dropped out of high school, I constantly lied to Alice and Harold Turnbough about how great my job was, while within me I hated the constant backstabbing tactics among the salesmen, the tension from the sales managers, and how utterly desperate I felt whenever I worked anybody who was "just looking." The Turnboughs were clueless about my stuntman fantasy. Nor did anyone know that I kept a pillowcase filled with clothes and enough cash to get me to Hollywood. Several times I had returned home from work so upset that I nearly ran off in the middle of the night. I wanted nothing more than to flee from my pathetic life. I had a craving to do something that wasn't overscrutinized, praying for a chance to take off and become part of the bright lights in the big city.

Part of me just didn't want to grow up, "be a man," and become responsible. As hard as my childhood was and as much as I had pushed myself to survive and move on, I began to have serious doubts about making it out there. As a teen there was a certain order of going to school and scurrying from job to job. Since I had planned every moment, I always knew what was around the next corner. Now, standing on the border to the next phase of my life, I realized knowing Paul and David and their relationships, how much I had missed when growing up as a child.

I suddenly felt naked and alone in a vast new world, compounded by the fact I didn't have an inkling of what lay ahead. Looking up at Mr. Marsh, I sniveled, "So what *do* I do?" As the words slipped, so did my quasi-fantasy of living a life of freewheeling adventures in Hollywood.

"Well, my young apprentice, that's the age-old question," The Sarge began. "I know it may seem a bit overwhelming right about now, but you'll be fine, *if* you keep your head on straight and get your act together. You're not going through anything that any of us *soon-to-be geriatrics* already haven't. It's a rite of passage. There's a big world out there and you can do anything. Follow your strength, *'use The Force,'* " Mike imitated from *Star Wars*. "You told me once you wanted to be a fireman. Well, go do it. Maybe the service would be a good place to get your feet wet in the pond of life. Sign up for a few years, see what you're made of, get an education beyond what any classroom can teach you. Hell, son, you can join the army, get your Jump Wings as a paratrooper, and maybe become a ranger. You could become a lean, mean, fightin' machine! Hell, look what it did for me!"

"Yeah," I jabbed, staring at the small bulge in his midsection.

"Back off, Slim, you're looking at a lot of years and a lot of beers. These eyes have seen a lot of adventure and soon enough you will too. Maybe we can check out what the army recruiter thinks your chances are. I might even put in a good word for you. No one likes a high school dropout, but we'll have to see what we can do. Here's a new set of maxims, and don't *even* ask what it means, look it up. Anyway, *Be all that you can be . . . the few, the brave, the proud. It's not just a job, but an adventure.* And finally . . . *Aim high.* Think about it!

"Thus endeth today's lesson," Mike smirked.

Ranger Marsh and I never made it down to the recruiter's office together, but between him and Dan, both men gave me a much deserved kick in the psychological backside. I *kinda* knew what I wanted to do with my life, but lacked the motivation to nudge myself forward. I was just too scared. My immediate short-term plan was one of sustenance. By pure coincidence I had an interview at another car dealership within a few days. I had to get that job. Next, as aggravating as I knew it was going to be, I had to get my GED. I had thought about returning to high school, but I was nearly half a year behind, and way too embarrassed to re-enroll as a failure in the slower classes, which would only make me farther behind, while still having to contend with earning a living full time in the adult workplace. With the short time I had left I was determined to get my act together. By the time I turned eighteen, if things weren't going too well, *then,* I told myself, I'd consider the military—if they'd have me. I saw enlisting as a last resort, even though it could fulfill a childhood dream of either becoming a fireman or living the adventure flying jets. My biggest fear was not only not passing their academic testing and the physical examinations, but the background checks that might reveal my severe childhood. By dropping out of school I had not only limited my employment options, but I had also stupidly painted myself into a corner.

Within a week I caught a lucky break. After my Vega's engine imploded, I was not only hired as a Chevy car salesman but the dealership loaned me a new truck! Within a few weeks I was back on top, selling cars and saving money while secretly studying reference books for my upcoming GED test. When I took my first weekend off, I drove back to Duinsmoore and blew the socks off The Sarge, Dan, and the other doubting Thomases when they saw my shiny new step-side brown truck. "Maybe I steered you wrong," Mr. Marsh conceded. "You more than appear to have a knack for the car barter business."

Paul and David were so impressed when on my next weekday off I proudly drove up to the high school—the same high school where I had been frisked for change while going to the bathroom—and picked them up when they planned to skip school after their second-period class. About an hour later, after I smashed the rear bumper into a pole, Paul advised me not to worry about the serious possibility of getting fired for wrecking the new truck since his father had a set of tools that would fix anything. As David and I sat in the back of the cab, Paul—with the seat pushed to its forward limit—did his best to drive over an abandoned, mud-infested hilly area, only to beach the Chevy truck in the thick bubbling ooze. As much as the three of us took turns trying everything possible to free the truck, we only ended up burying the back end more. When the late morning faded into mid afternoon, I began to worry when Paul and David stated they would soon be forced to abandon me to return home. I began to fear being stranded without food or water throughout the night, but then some passerby in a heavier truck pulled us free. The moment Paul, David, and I returned to Duinsmoore, I pestered Paul about the tools he said would fix the truck. When my friend brushed me off, I yelled, naively believing that Dan would suddenly drop everything and instantly fix the damaged bumper, as well as paint the grazed side of the truck, to

166

perfection, free of charge, *and* all within a matter of a few minutes.

The next day, with my head lowered in shame, I confessed to the concerned managers at the dealership that I had somehow accidentally struck a pole while carefully backing up. They bought it. For among the group of high-strung, caffeine-addicted, chain-smoking, down-and-out, unreliable sales staff, I appeared extremely shy, professionally composed, and clean-cut, never missing a day of work, while selling a fair amount of cars. Because I didn't go out, drink, smoke, or indulge in any normal, everyday vices, no one suspected my opposite unrestrained life with my two friends. However, after another series of *incidents* that paralleled every time I visited Duinsmoore, the dealership became very concerned of the damage to their small fleet and threatened to fire me, as well as financial retribution, unless I sold a certain quota per week.

Yet part of me *still* couldn't help myself. At work I was intensely focused to the point of being overly stoic, but during my rare time off, the moment I drove through Menlo Park and turned from Bay Road onto Duinsmoore Way, a carefree adventurous persona took over. One Friday afternoon, after working the opening shift and having the rare luck of selling a car to a person who was just looking, I was rewarded by my manager with a brand-new Camaro for the weekend. After the group of men at Dan's garage spent a few seconds gawking at my latest acquisition, and failing to rally David to join me because of his after-school job, Paul and I cruised through the back streets, admiring the celebritylike mansions. Within a few minutes of trying to pump Paul for any form of conversation, I became frustrated. A few minutes before at Duinsmoore, Paul's eyes seemed to shine with anticipation of the next exploration in adventure, but sitting beside me now he seemed cold and withdrawn. By the time we reached the side road that paralleled my old high school, I huffed, "Okay, out with it. What's the deal?"

Paul gestured toward Menlo-Atherton High. "*That's* the deal. School sucks."

Without any thought, I surprised myself by instantly replying, "I agree, but so what? School always sucks. What's the prob'?"

Paul shook his head as he crossed his arms against his chest. "You don't get it. I hate going there. The classes are boring, the teachers suck 'cause they're too busy trying to run classes that have become zoos. I get mugged like two, three times a week. I get picked on 'cause I'm short. I hate it. I hate it all, I hate everything about it, man. It totally sucks!"

"Man. I thought I was the only dude that got mugged. Did they take you while you were in the bathroom?" I asked.

"Man, I get picked on all the time, everywhere, just because I'm short and am way smarter than like half the goofs in the classes who act like animals and don't want to learn anything anyway. Then, by the time the teachers get the class quiet, the period's almost over, so what's the use. I tell my parents, but they brush me off. No one gets it, man," Paul stated.

I shook my head. For Paul to open up like this was a big deal. "I don't know what to say, except everybody goes through it. Maybe not the same thing, but everybody goes through something."

"No, man, *you don't get it.* I get beat up. I can't walk through the hallways; I can't go to the bathroom to go take a leak; I can't do anything."

"Me either," I replied. "The same shit happens to me. The exact same thing and I thought, ya know, I was the only one. But it ain't so. And when I get picked on, and I don't mean teased or harassed, I mean I get slaughtered every day. In junior high I must have gone through four or five dozen pairs of glasses. I got creamed 'cause I was the new kid, 'the foster kid,' who didn't fit in, had four eyes, was too skinny, too geeky, I stuttered, I mumbled, said the wrong thing at the wrong time. I never stood up for myself and when I did, I wasn't supposed to. I didn't have the cool clothes or any real friends, and I can't tell you how alone I felt. Every single day."

Paul continued to stew. "No, it's different now." But I shook my head in disagreement. "And whatever you do, don't lecture me. I get enough of that from home. They can't even talk to me. My mom just thinks if I sit down and watch some ABC Afterschool Special on TV about drug addiction, teen pregnancy, or the dangers of getting into a car with strangers, it will, like, solve all my problems. They treat me like I'm still a little kid. I can't talk to them. They didn't get mugged at school. They didn't have to deal with all the crap that goes on in the classroom. Even when they ask,

'How was your day in school?,' they don't really want to know. I can't talk to them."

"I know what you mean," I agreed. "I can't really talk to my foster parents on some things. And don't ask me where I learned about the opposite sex from. You know, it's kinda weird. I mean, I love my foster parents, the Turnboughs, but at times I feel I can talk more to Mike and Sandy Marsh about that stuff, or to your dad on other things, than anybody else. Maybe it's that whole breaking away thing—the more we try to pull away, the more they try to control us and corral us in. I dunno." I took a deep breath before confessing, "And I don't care if you hate me for saying this, but I love your dad."

Paul rolled his eyes. "*Everybody* says that, but you don't live with him."

I quickly cut Paul off. "And you don't live in my world. If everyone loves your dad, then chances are he's pretty cool. If I had a dad, I'd wish . . ."

"I can't tell you how many times David and everybody else says that about him," Paul interjected.

I reached my boiling point with Paul. "Then shut the hell up and listen, man! Your dad's awesome, and your mom, well, she scares the hell out of me but she's only protecting her family. You have no idea what it's like out there!" I said, sounding like Mr. Marsh just a short time ago. "And I know at times life seems like a bitch and all, but you've pretty much got it made in the shade. There's so much crap out there, I can't even begin to tell you. At least your dad's not some drunk and your mom's not some psycho with the sole intention of trying to kill you."

"You don't know what goes on in my house," Paul countered. "It ain't all tea and cookies."

"I do know a good thing when I see it. So why the attitude? Ever since I've known you . . ."

"Sometimes I hate it. I hate it all. Home, school, everything."

I lowered my voice, whining like a baby. "Oh, so what ya gonna do? Drop out of school and run away from home?"

Paul raised a finger at me. "Look who's talking. You quit. And it was you that was talking about going off to Hollywood."

Suddenly I felt ten years older. The Hollywood thing seemed like a long time ago. "Yeah, you're right, the stuntman thing *was* my idea, but it was just some stupid run off and join the circus thing. And you wanna know who saved my bacon on that one?" Paul just looked at me, already knowing the answer. "Yeah, that's right, your dad and Mr. Marsh. My own foster parents didn't have a clue of how many times I came so close to splitting. All because life sucks.

"Thank God for your dad and The Sarge," I continued. "There's people who wouldn't give me the time of day and these guys cared enough to tell me like it is. It just made me think, that's all. They didn't tell me what to do, but made me really think."

"Everybody's telling me what to do," Paul responded.

"Go to church, become an altar boy, get good grades, join NASA."

"So?" I shook my head.

"So, I'm always being told what to do and I'm sick of it!"

I had to laugh. "I know, that's the thing that sucks, but it never ends. I've always been pushed around, bullied around, ordered around at home and at work. It's just life. Half the time I don't fight it and just do it, so I don't get so stressed out. But that's my point: You have folks who care enough about you to give you the time of day. It's different for a lot of other kids like me. When I'm eighteen, I'm out on my own, but even if you screw up, you'll always have a place to call home. No matter what you do or whatever kind of jam you get into, you'll always have your mom and dad." I swallowed hard before I stated the one thing to Paul that I held back since I had first met him. "I'm sure you've heard this from David, but I'll tell it to your face: I'd kill to have a father and a family like yours. I'd climb any mountain, I'd crawl on shards of glass, I'd go to hell and back, I'd do whatever it took to be a member of your family, the Howards, the Marshes, or any other family on Duinsmoore. Everyone's always telling me how naive and inept I am, and maybe that's true, but I know enough to know your family is it. I've been through some crazy shit, and I'm here to tell you, my own brothers and I would switch places with you in a heartbeat."

Paul lowered his arms and sat still while I wound down. "On the school thing: You're right, I messed up. Out of all the things I've done, well, that's the worst. But it's different for me. I'm almost eighteen and I gotta work 'cause I'll be out on my own. I shoulda studied. I shoulda applied myself, but it's kind of a bitch putting in all those hours at work, then going to school trying to learn fractions.

"But it's different for you, Paul. Okay, school sucks and your folks drive you batty, but you have a home, you're not being bounced around from place to place. Don't you get it? You don't have to wake up every day thinking, is this the day that your mom flips out and snaps your neck. It's different for guys like me. You're always saying how I make a big deal every time I come to Duinsmoore, well, now you know why.

"It's no one's fault, it's just different. And you're smart, and I mean brilliant. You're like the Einstein of Menlo Park. Everywhere I go, it's always 'Paul, Paul, Paul.' Maybe your folks have high expectations for you 'cause you have this gift, this brilliance that Howie sure as hell doesn't have and what makes me feel like a retard in front of you at times. Howard and I talk, we talk a lot, and we know how this is all gonna go down. David's probably gonna go into construction. Me, hell, after working with these old burned-out salesmen with big bellies and frayed rayon shirts and who live in some crappy upstairs studio apartment, I'll probably get a job sweeping floors, and that's okay by me. But you, you, Paul, if you don't use your gift . . . well . . . that would be the biggest tragedy of all."

I could feel pent-up pressure from within my chest begin to ease. Surprised with all that I had said, I looked at Paul, who sat completely dumbfounded. "For a guy who used to get nervous and stutter, you sure can be a wind-bag," Paul stated. I shook my head at the same realization. "Maybe you can be one of those traveling preachers or one of those Zig Ziglar types."

I huffed at Paul's statement. At one point I thought that, as much as I had lambasted my sensitive friend, he would have either flipped me off, become a statue, or fled from the car. Now, for a moment, both of us just sat in the car, looking at each other. As much as I loved Paul, in some way I was also jealous of all that was placed before him. I only hoped that whatever he kept to himself didn't eat at him and spoil his chances of going for his dreams. With the shiny Camaro idling in front of a fork in the road, Paul and I weren't sure which direction to go.

10

Stepping Out

I couldn't believe I, of all people, after all the gigantic blunders I had made in my life, had leaned on someone, let alone one of my best friends and basically told him to get over it, appreciate his blessings, and grow the hell up. I surprised myself on how adamant I was to Paul, who may have thought he had it pretty rough. As I lectured him, the words seemed more like those coming from either his father, the Marshes, or the legion of my concerned apprehensive foster parents. Even though on some things I felt I had a good head on my shoulders when it came to some of the pitfalls and temptations of teenage life, whenever I received a stern lecture from anybody way over my age group, I felt they didn't know what it was like for me and were overly sensitive over nothing. As a teen I felt that at times it was an *us* against *them* situation: "the sky is falling" adults versus "well, if it does let's see what happens" youth. Yet, after disclosing to Paul how good he had it, I wondered if I had somehow inched over to the other side. As frustrated as I was with my friend at times, I hoped he would not follow the path of some of the dozens upon dozens of foster kids I had known, who, for one reason or another, had thrown up their hands and quit on themselves or adopted an "I'll show them. No one's gonna tell me what to do!" attitude. While some of them probably had every right to initially rebel after all the crap they endured, I prayed that my brilliant friend, with all the assets he had, was smart enough not to travel that path. By sticking my neck out and telling Paul like it was, I felt I was upholding our Rules of Engagement—if one of us fell down, the other must pick him up.

With the air cleared between us, Paul and I continued to idle the Chevy Camaro through the sides street of Menlo Park. Yet within a few minutes of my "pull yourself up by your bootstraps and show some gratitude" sermon, we once again simultaneously diverted from maturity when we stopped a few feet in front of an inclined set of railroad tracks. "Remember that movie . . ." I began.

". . . when the car jumped over the tracks . . ." Paul flashed a rare smile as I nodded in agreement. Then as if activating his high-speed internal computer, Einstein, Jr., instantly calculated what it would take to approach the incline and "fly" up and over the railroad tracks. Paul's summation seemed so elementary: Back up several hundred feet, floor the accelerator, and see what happens. The only oddity that Paul insisted on was, rather than approach the slope head-on, do it at a slight angle. In this way, my friend deduced, this method would prevent the heavily weighted front end of our Chevy from somehow bottoming out from the hurling airborne speed.

But I still had a few concerns, ranging from safety to any possible damage, as well as financial and legal liabilities. "But," I raised my finger while thinking out loud, "we now have the *driving* ROEs that will see us through!" Paul, rubbing his chin, most certainly agreed that, before any activity commenced, ensure no law enforcement agency is within "The Area of Operation." Second, ensure that The Area of Operation is clear of any and all children/civilians. Third, for reasons of safety, make certain there is sufficient clearance in front of the driver at all times. And, lastly, reverify checklist, take a deep breath, say a quick prayer, and think about what you're getting yourself into. Just as the initial ROEs the three of us initiated in Dan's garage had assisted us all those years, the new driving ROEs again kept Paul, David, and I from straying *too far* on the wild side.

With my right foot pumping the gas pedal, while my left one maintained pressure on the brakes, I shouted to Paul to initiate the prelaunch checklist.

"Parking brake off?" Paul asked.

Looking down and to the left, I could see the brake pedal was not set. "Roger, brake off."

"Check for bogies."

"Radar is clear of any police and any law enforcement entities."

"Clear of women, children, and civilians?"

"Roger," I replied, "I have a visual; all is clear."

"Reverify checklist."

Once again I mentally and visually ran down the checklist. The only anomaly I noted out loud was, "I'm noticing a patch of fog on the other side of the tracks. . . ."

"Noted," Paul chimed in.

"Clear left, clear rear, clear forward," I said in final preparation.

"Roger. Clear right, clear rear, clear forward. I concur," Paul stated. "Let her rip!"

I took a deep breath, held it, and squeezed my butt cheeks together, while clutching the leather steering wheel. With my foot planted firmly on the brake pedal, I began to slowly apply more pressure to the gas pedal. "On my command . . ." Paul ordered, ". . . in five . . . four . . . three . . . release brakes . . . one . . . Punch it!"

Obeying my mission control copilot, I released the brakes, which unlocked the rear wheels as I floored the accelerator at the precise moment, forcing the back of the car to swerve wildly to the right as the car shot forward. "Apply rudder control," Paul barked.

"Copy," I replied, before easing off the gas, which alleviated most of the shifting momentum. But now my main concern was proper alignment of the car, for the incline and the tracks were nearly upon us.

"More to the left," the copilot advised.

"Roger," I flatly responded, as I nudged the Camaro to the right before aligning the entire car to the left.

"No, no, no!" Paul countered. "I said left, not right, but more left!"

"I got it!" I said, brushing Paul off, knowing I had to correct more to the right, *then* realign my take-off point, so we didn't land too far to the left and beyond the pavement and into someone's front yard. After making a slight course correction I now had the perfect visual launch point and the car exactly where I wanted it. As the Chevy abruptly pitched up from the incline, my brain suddenly processed everything in slow motion. I looked over at Paul and uttered as if in some echo chamber, "Seat belts . . . did we ever say anything about seat belts . . . ?" Paul's eyes widened as if to say *ooohhh . . . noooooooooo!* but it was too late. The roaring sound of the engine ceased momentarily as the car leapt into the air. For a few split seconds Paul and I were free from the earth's gravitational pull as Paul's body casually floated to the ceiling like some Apollo astronaut, while my stash of pencils, pens, sheets of paper, and car brochures hovered, too, before sailing wildly in every direction.

By the time my eyes readjusted back outside, the front end of the car crashed into the pavement. Before I could fire off a snappy one-liner critique to Paul on his landing miscalculation, the back end of the Chevy followed, forcing both ends of the car to wallow from its weight. By the third bounce I could see we were now in serious trouble. Not only was the Camaro on the wrong side of the road, but the edges of the left tires were in a soft ditch, and I feared the weight and the speed coupled with the left tires' slippage would flip the car over. As if to protect myself from impending doom, I wanted to suck in a deep breath and tighten every fiber of every muscle, but instead yelled over to my copilot, "Brace, brace, brace!" Once again, as I had years ago when I thought I was going to splatter little Amy Neyland with my minibike, my mind spun with options, but bringing the car to a screeching halt was not one of them. Nor did I believe I had the luxury of time to carefully ease off the gas pedal and allow the car's momentum to come to rest, for I could feel the car being pulled by the invisible inertia and toward the ditch. The only remedy that came to mind was to snap the Camaro to the right, praying the speed and the sudden jolt would force the car out of the trench and back onto the safety of the pavement. As I jerked the steering wheel to the right, and as the car came out from the ditch, I felt a small bump from under the left side of the Camaro. Suddenly time stood still. When I glanced over at Paul, he appeared smaller, as he was squashed against his bucket seat. While trying to process another possible dilemma, the equilibrium from my ears told me something was not as it should be. The car seemed fine, but as I steered it straight ahead the handling seemed a little odd.

In a low-pitched, squeaky voice, Paul uttered the words, *"Two wheels. You're . . . driving . . . the car . . . on two wheels. . . ."* My heart froze. My fingers became glued to the steering wheel, as I tried not to breathe—thinking my exhaled breath would somehow tumble the Camaro over. When Paul repeated his observation, I glanced down at him, seeing just how close his head and his right shoulder were in relation to the road that blazed past him just a few feet away. Carefully turning my head toward the front of the car, I could make out two odd-shaped, off-centered white dots approaching my path. From my high altitude I thought how funny the white specks looked and why they were on *my* side of the road . . . unless? Before I could utter a syllable, Paul—the ever-so-cool, calm and collected—instructed, "If you would, please, steer a little to the right. Just . . . just a tad. Don't overthink it, but a tad to the right." As I nudged the steering wheel, I prayed my hands didn't suddenly slip from the pools of sweat collecting on my palms. As I applied the slightest pressure on the hypersensitive steering wheel, I could feel the left side of the car wobble as the right-side tires began to squeal. When the other car ahead hesitantly drove past our Chevy, I had had more excitement than my nearly soiled pants could stand, so I made a sudden move to the left. Before I could yell out another command of, "Brace, brace, brace . . ." the Camaro bounced once before settling, as if nothing had happened, except for the fact that somehow the linkage to the transmission shift became broken, locking the mechanism in first gear.

By the time Paul and I limped back to his house, David stood outside like an excited puppy. "Cool car, dude. Let's go for a ride and cruise the Strip. The chicks will definitely dig us now."

"Too late," I broke out in a laugh.

David shook his head as he slid into the cockpit of the Camaro, inspecting the multiple gauges and playing with the newest, chicest device known to car audio—the eight-track tape player. "What's wrong? You need money for gas or something?"

Standing in the middle of Dan's driveway, Paul and I relived the entire episode, explaining in detail how everything that happened was not only intended but professionally executed, as if my friend and I had re-created the same scene from the James Bond film *Diamonds Are Forever* in which Agent 007 casually piloted his fire-engine red, Mach-1 Ford Mustang on two wheels while evading those wishing him harm.

Afterward all David could blurt out was, "No way! For real? You mean, the car's broken?" David asked in confusion while now checking for any dents or scratches. "It's brand-new and only has . . . forty-four miles?" All I could do was shuffle my feet while admitting yes. "You mean to tell me you've had this car for four hours and it's already trashed? That's, like, a record." I nodded yes, while feeling as if I was being scolded. But then David broke out in a wide smile. "Cool!"

I didn't think it was so cool and neither did my bosses at the car dealership, who were far less understanding and much more expressive in their displeasure. Yet, with no visual damage to the car, I fabricated a tale on how I was casually driving at night, on a darkened street, when . . . I hit a series of potholes . . . and . . . somehow . . . the transmission linkage simply broke. Displaying confidence rather than fear, I quickly added, "Good thing it was me driving the car and not some customer; otherwise they might sue or, worse, demand a recall of the other Camaros!"

With no evidence of misbehavior, I was lightly scolded

and semithreatened with unemployment unless I sold another allotment of cars. Over the weeks that followed, I somehow fulfilled my manager's quotient of sales and in the process, much to everyone's surprise, especially mine, I was awarded salesman of the month. To upper management's horror, I was presented with keys to the ultimate prize: a glistening black Corvette with removable T-tops. But before I could drive off, the owner—who I'd never seen making an appearance at the dealership before—pulled me aside, promising me death by peeling off every layer of my skin if I came back next week with even bird droppings on the car. That evening as I drove home to the Turnboughs, in the far right-hand lane at five miles below the posted speed limit, I prayed that when I parked the car I wouldn't scratch, dent, or dismember the extra-wide, extra-high wheel wells on the car, that made it practically impossible to park the Corvette.

The only thing separating my grand arrival to Duinsmoore as if I were Caesar returning to Rome after years of victorious battles was that I had been banned from the neighborhood for two weeks. The Sunday before receiving the Corvette, after eating dinner with the Howards, David and I convinced his parents that the two of us would spend a few hours at Paul's house. At the same time, Paul convinced Dan and Beth that he would spend a few hours at David's home. Moments later, outside in the cover of darkness, the three of us giggled like kindergarten kids as Paul steered my loaned Chevy step-side truck while David and

I, in stealth, pushed the truck down the block before climbing in, in search of new adventures that somehow went awry. Hours later upon our return, I surprised myself by having the idea of shutting off the truck motor, to elude any noise and pilot the truck on its own momentum. I felt pretty sure that Paul's and David's parents would be none the wiser . . . until I strained my eyes to see a pair of silhouettes . . . ghostlike figures standing in the middle of the street, covered within a swirl of grayish fog, with their hands glued to their hips. With a rush of adrenaline still surging from our latest exploit, I nearly burst, "Hey, guys, do you see what I see?"

Beside me I could feel Paul's body tighten. "Oh my God!"

"Holy crap!" David replied. "It's the Moms!"

Nothing I had faced came close to the fury of the two mothers who unleashed every syllable of every phrase of every unkind word in the history of the English language at the three of us. Slumping their shoulders, Paul and David suddenly acted as if I had, against their own will, kidnapped them as part of some deviant plot to my diabolical scheme. Only afterward, as I motored away, did I feel any sense of justice when I saw Mrs. Brazell lead Paul into their home while clamping her fingers onto his ear, and while David endured a lungful of Mrs. Howard's nonstop high-pitched verbal assault.

Now, upon returning to Duinsmoore, the Corvette and I did not receive praise, let alone oohs and aahs, from a single person on the block. Even Sandy Marsh, who adored Corvettes and had never been for a ride in one, was only mildly impressed. I could only guess that Sandy had still been upset with *me*—which kept *her* from enjoying the car. After a brief visit with my friends, who were stuck within the confines of their own parental penitentiary, the guilt of cruising around in a black sports car while blaring the eight-track tape player spread to me like a cold. The next day I flung the Corvette's keys onto the sales manager's desk—without an explanation, and without a single nick.

Overall, the car wasn't for me. Sure, for anyone else it was, "a babe magnet." But not me. I had to practically beg a girl I knew in high school, promising to take her to a fancy Bay Area restaurant. At dinner I became so nervous that my eyes kept twitching, while I stuttered through a non-stop set of apologies for my sudden inflection. Later that evening after spending my paycheck, I didn't feel so cool as I escorted my date back to her parents' front door while fantasizing the much anticipated good-night kiss, and suddenly tripping on the walkway, falling flat on my face, giving myself a bloody nose. With one hand covering my leaky nose, all I could do was shake her hand with my other one. The whole status thing of the Corvette made me too paranoid of wrecking it. Even when zipping down the highway, I couldn't relax; I just knew everyone was trying to crash into me.

While I admired the mysterious world of girls, my only ambition now was to study during the slow part of the day at work in order to pass my upcoming GED. With every day, I learned not only how foolish I was, but also how on the mark Dan and Mike had been. The whole car sales thing, while fun for a while, was not for me.

Expanding my day-to-day education, I became engrossed in newspapers to truly understand the depths of the country's recession and the magnitude of gas prices shooting to record highs. Then, when the management announced that due to slow sales the dealership could no longer offer demos for the staff to drive, I knew it was only a matter of time. But I needed a car, so spending as little as possible I purchased a horrible-looking, fourteen-year-old Ford Mustang whose underpowered six-cylinder engine was in need of a major overhaul. But I didn't care; just as long as it got me from point A to point B, that was more than enough for me. Feeling confident about my upcoming GED test, I randomly circled a date on the calendar and when that Friday arrived, by a stroke of luck I sold two cars in the morning, then proudly walked into the manager's office to proclaim the end of my career in car sales. The men were so stunned, completely speechless, as I hopped into my dilapidated, oxidized-orange car before proudly sputtering down the endless rows of dealerships that covered the avenue.

My plan was simple: Pass the GED, then beg, barter, and, if necessary, beg some more on my way into the U.S. Air Force. After two attempts and feeling a little more humbled I finally passed the high school equivalency test. Within minutes I raced over to the recruiter's office to flash my paperwork in front of the overly stoic sergeant's face. Months before I hung up my job at the car dealership, I began

spending my off time planted next to the reluctant recruiter's desk, retaining every brochure, watching every
video, over and over again, while memorizing any paper
that I could get my fingers on. Now with my GED, and after filling out endless reams of paperwork, I was well on
the road to enlisting in the service and beginning my journey into adulthood. Yet, the closer I came to completing the
necessary forms, the more I worried about my past being
exposed. The issue came to a head when a senior master
sergeant scanned through my list of different addresses.
Tilting his head down, the recruiter growled, "Are you one
of those foster kids, boy?" While doing my best attempt to
stand in a mock attention stance, I answered yes. "What'd
you do to become a foster kid? You got a problem with au-
thority? Well, do ya . . . boy?" I shook my head no. While he
continued to stare right through me, I began to count to
myself, knowing that this man held my future. After thinking, praying, and planning, and after all the stupid blunders I'd gotten myself into, the service was my only path to
pull myself together. By the time I had counted to twelve, I
knew my chances had evaporated. I let out a sigh, and as
my rigid posture slumped, the grim-faced sergeant snatched
a black government pen from his desk and signed my
papers.

Within weeks I had passed every hurdle and was finally
offered a slot to enlist. As excited as I was to begin my new
life, I felt I needed a week to tie up any loose ends. First on
my list was the Turnboughs. While I thought they had no

187

idea of what I was up to, I was surprised to find out they had known my plans all along. Alice and Harold, who had been through so much with me, felt relieved that I had done something positive for my future, and their only concern was, "Are you going to tell your parents?"

Leaning back in my seat, where I was only moments ago fidgeting nervously, thinking how I was going to break the news, I now flashed a rare smile. "I just did. . . . Mother, Father, I'm joining the air force. I leave next week."

A couple of days prior to flying off to basic training, The Sarge asked if I'd drop by to say good-bye. Thinking ahead I crammed my precious belongings—a quadraphonic eight-track tape player sound system and my priceless, rolled-up James Bond promotional movie posters that had covered every inch of my old room—into my old Mustang and prayed the car would somehow limp its way to Duinsmoore one last time. Making the final left turn into Suburban Park, I slowed the vehicle to a crawl, inching my way toward Mike and Sandy's house. As I had years ago when I first moved into the neighborhood, I could still hear the sound of the gentle breeze from the huge trees that hung over the immaculate sidewalks that led to the manicured lawns of the majestic-like homes. In all the endless weekends, no matter how high-strung Paul, David, and I may have appeared to act, I never once failed to stop and appreciate the serenity of Duinsmoore.

Bringing my squeaky car to a stop in front of famed Marsh Manor, I was taken aback when The Sarge greeted

me in combat fatigues and a military Airborne beret, followed in unison by his junior squad members, William and
Eric, attired in their own set of camo' gear, with little Eric
sporting an Aussie hat while clutching a cork-string pop
rifle. It was only after I spied Dan walking across the street,
dressed in a female hillbilly outfit showing off his knobby
knees and blacked-out teeth, with Paul and David behind
him in their own quasi-Boy Scout/commando gear, did I
understand that dropping by was a going-away party. Stepping into their house, Sandy greeted me with a hug, while
my unofficial stepmom of the block, Mrs. Howard, thrust an
enormous care package into my hands. It took several moments for me to comprehend all the balloons, streamers,
and banners that engulfed the same living room where I
had spent so many hours devouring books on aircraft and
that had somehow helped propel me into the next era of
my life.

With the house filled to capacity with practically everyone from the block, and the harmony of Leon Redbone re-
verberating throughout the living room, I couldn't help but
stand in a corner and marvel at everything, as if my vision
was like a movie camera taking in all the activity in slow
motion. How everyone was smiling and laughing in their
small groups, nibbling on snacks, or taking sips from their
drinks while the kids darted in every direction. I had always sensed it, but now, within hours of my departure, I
discovered the secret of Duinsmoore. It wasn't simply a
block with rows of homes nudged next to each other, but a
neighborhood that became its own family. And family was

the single thing I had craved since my crazed, alcoholic mother had *exiled* me from my own household years before I was removed and placed into foster care. And I appreciated all that my foster parents did for me, but because of my constant placements—being moved from home to home—I felt I truly couldn't bond. But that was the gift that Duinsmoore gave me, that sense of belonging I so yearned for my whole life.

As the party began to peak, The Doc Savage of Duinsmoore took center stage. "While this may appear to be a going-away party for America's newest inductee of the armed forces, it's really a celebration that we are finally rid of you. . . ."

"Damn right!" Mr. Ballow sarcastically bellowed.

"However, in all seriousness, I can state as Chancellor of Security of Duinsmoore that upon your initial arrival the block has never been the same, and may not likely recover from what can only be described as excessive psychological damage. My case in point being our good neighbor Mr. Brazell," Dan suddenly curtsied to the howling crowd, "who has become so deranged that he has taken up cross-dressing for what would surely be because of hiding his emotional scars that you and your band of merry men have instilled to him."

"Hear, hear!" a small group chanted.

"As taxpayers, patriots, and veterans, it is our fond hope that if there is another shooting war, that the air force in all its wisdom will have enough sense to drop you behind enemy lines and have you promote chaos against the said enemy at will, as you have against us. God forbid if they hand any utensil other than a spatula; for if they do, I will commandeer my family from the Golden State, and it is my intention to hide them in the remotest part within the mountains of Bolivia.

"But in all seriousness," Mike continued while maintaining a grasp on his frothed beer, "for those of us whom have dared to know you, we realize you've been through a lot, and in some aspects we are proud how far you've come and am hopeful of your future. Now," Mike stopped to clear his throat, "does anyone here have any parting words of advice for our young Airman Extraordinaire?"

"Keep your mouth shut and learn to become invisible," someone yelled.

"Never volunteer for KP duty," another boomed.

"When you go overseas, don't drink the water."

"Stay away from all brothels, bordellos, and geisha houses."

"Always wear your raincoat."

Suddenly Sandy Marsh blushed at the next comment, which I didn't understand: "That's right, Airman, always remember," The Sarge thundered, "keep your gun clean at all times. Travel to exotic places, take in the sites, and explore your world. You're in the thick of it now, son!"

Minutes later, when I realized it was the first party that anyone had ever thrown for me, I cried inside. I slipped outside and stood near the same spot where I had first introduced myself to Paul and David such a long time ago. And, as if on cue, both young men stumbled from the party to meet me. Paul, with his shoulders slumped, seemed up-set. "What's wrong?" I asked.

Before Paul could reply, David interjected, "Oh, he's just pissed 'cause Dan wouldn't let him strap on his gun for the party."

"The .357?" I swallowed.

"Yeah, it would have been cool. Then if someone got out of line, I could've blasted 'em," Paul emphasized, as if his hand were the Magnum revolver.

With raised eyebrows David and I looked at each other. "Why do I get this sinking feeling I'm leaving, only to find out that one day you're in some tower shooting at people. You know, Paul, we really have to work on your attitu . . ." But before I could finish my lecture, Susie Neyland materi-alized. With gaping mouths the three of us stood perfectly still. No one dared to breathe. When she made eye contact with Paul and David, Miss Neyland stopped in stride for a mere nanosecond to give the boys a wave. Susie may have gestured to me as well, but by habit, and stupidly, I snapped my neck down to avoid gazing at the Princess of Duinsmoore, thus avoiding the near-certain possibility of making a jerk of myself for all to enjoy. Yet for the briefest of moments, with my eyes closed I could see Susie again strutting down the same street, only now in a short skirt, and a clingy white blouse tied at her tan waist, while all the while smiling at *me*, as if I were the only person on the planet. Then to the dismay of everyone from the block who lined both sides of the sidewalks, The Princess stopped in front of me, stood on her toes, and planted a deep, long passionate kiss on me, while we both held each other. Afterward, with glistening eyes, *my Susie* purred, "Come back in one piece, soldier boy." But, after opening my eyes back to reality, Susie sauntered past, commenting that she was looking for her father. Paul leaped at the chance to volunteer his services. David and I again stared at each other in mock confusion before simultaneously chanting, *"Paul and Susie sittin' in a tree . . . K-I-S-S-I-N-G! First comes love, then comes marriage, then comes Paul with the baby carriage!"*

"Man," I commented when the effects wore off, "she is such a fox."

"Then go up and talk to her."

"Why, so I could show her how well I can stutter like the village idiot? Besides, she doesn't even know I'm alive."

"Oh, yes she does," David commented. "Remember Amy's her baby sister. They all know you quite well. Besides, I thought you had a thing for Paul's sister, Dori?"

"Definitely." I shook my head. "I lust for Susie, but love Dori." David shook his head, indicating he didn't follow. "Okay, here's the plan: Even though Dori doesn't know me either . . . though she did say hello to me once . . . no, maybe twice . . . anyway, I eventually woo her . . ."

"Woo?!" Howard laughed.

"Shut up, man. This is it. This is, like, my master plan. Eventually, Dori likes me enough to get married, I buy a place for her on Duinsmoore. Dan could be, like, my dad, and you, my pimple-infested friend, not Paul, marries Susie, and Paul ends up with your sister, and we all live here and, you know, live happily . . ."

"... ever after," David finished. "But I thought you told me you wanted to find your real dad and live at the Russian River?" Howard stopped to have his thoughts catch up with him. "You're just kidding, aren't you, about all of us living here with the girls and that living happily ever after stuff? You're pullin' my leg." I smiled yes. "But it was a cool idea," David grinned back. "Man, I'd give anything to see Paul's mom put her arm around you at your wedding and call you 'son'!"

"Can you imagine our genetic offspring running amok on Duinsmoore? A generation of chaos and calamity," I said in perfect rhythm and timing.

"You are definitely sounding like The Sarge."

"I didn't when I first moved here, but every once in a while I have my moments."

Seconds passed while David and I stood in silence. "This is it?"

I looked up at David, squinting my eyes from the sun's descending glare. "Yep, I reckon. But not to worry, you'll still be my bud," I joked.

"You aren't gonna move back here, are you?" David asked in a serious tone.

"Nope," I shook my head. "It's just the last of a childhood fantasy. Susie, Dori, Dan, the Marshes, Paul, you, and I, living here forever was something to keep me from stepping out there," I pointed toward the horizon, "in the wild blue yonder. I know sometimes I say stuff and do things that are stupid, but I always knew what I had to do. I was just too afraid to do it."

David's face softened, "I don't want you to go. When you go . . . I gotta grow up, too."

"Come on, you still have a couple of years before the big one-eight," I consoled. "You and Paul are gonna have a blast."

David shoved his hands in his pockets while shuffling his feet. "Mr. Marsh says Iran's gonna explode. Says the Middle East, that's gonna be the next big thing."

I shook my head in disagreement. "Listen, the last thing the air force is going to do is give me a gun. Can you imagine that? Spaz Boy, the Barney Fife of Duinsmoore with a gun? Come on, man, you know me, I'd probably screw up and shoot myself in the foot or get my squad captured or killed. If they ever become that desperate, then we're in some serious trouble. Besides, the air force flies jets and drops bombs. They're not the rangers or the marines. I'm gonna be fine." I paused to gaze back at my friend, who seemed less apprehensive.

"And *that's* what I'm trying to tell you!" I said as David shot me a puzzled look. "That's the one thing you, your mom, Paul, the Marshes, Dan, and this neighborhood gave me. You all taught me to live and not to agonize about every goddamn thing that may or may not happen to me. As asininely stupid as this sounds, all the crazy stuff we all did together taught me to be less robotic and step out and take a chance. But the big thing, the one thing you two gave me . . ." I stopped to take in a breath of air and to make sure I didn't break down. ". . . Paul and you gave me a second chance at being a kid . . ." I stopped midsentence, surprised at my own revelation. ". . . And for that I cannot begin to tell you how grateful I am. Thanks, David. Thanks for being *my friend*." I turned away before he saw me cry. "Before I met you guys, I never thought I was going make it to twenty. Maybe that's why I worked myself to death before I came here. This place represents everything that's right in the world. Thanks for always being there for me."

The next morning after spending the night on the Marshes' sofa, I said my good-byes to Mike, Sandy, and the boys before they scrambled out the door. Strolling down the street to the Howards', I repeatedly knocked on their door, but no one answered. With a quick sigh I ambled up the block to Paul's home to pay my respects to my friend and the man I regarded as a father, but the Brazell family had also left for the day. Standing in the middle of the street, I closed my eyes and leaned back spreading my arms toward the clear blue sky. Opening my eyes, the scent of jasmine didn't seem to fill my senses as before, and now the block seemed more like an abandoned town from the Wild West than the Disneyland utopia it was for me the evening before. Reluctantly, I walked over to my car, half praying it wouldn't start, half praying that I wouldn't have to transcend into adulthood. As excited as I was for the adventures just hours away, part of me wanted to slither back into the Marshes' abode and burrow myself within a thick warm blanket and never come out. To my surprise the Mustang fired up on its first try, as if wanting to take me to my next journey. As I slowly drove down the street, a small stream rolled down my cheek. With Duinsmoore in my rearview mirror, I said a prayer for all those I loved so deeply. I then thanked God for showing me a piece of heaven on earth and for allowing me the absolute time of my life.

Epilogue

Within weeks of my departure, the spirit of Duinsmoore faded. By Indian Summer of 1979, The Doc Savage of Duinsmoore and his family had had enough of the Bay Area's overcrowding, while barely making ends meet, so they packed up and fled to the great region outside of his hometown of Denver to reside in a bigger, modern house. No longer did they need to struggle as much as they had for years in California's rat race.

The Suburban Park Association never recovered. While I was on military leave that Christmas, visiting Paul, David and Dan, the afternoon garage gatherings seemed almost lifeless. At first I thought that I may have been one of the reasons for the monotony, since I was—through the baptism of adulthood—now tolerated within the fold. And, by sheer coincidence, I had just completed military training school in Denver, allowing me to spend my weekend time with the Marsh family, and because I had all the "Intel" on

The Sarge, I instantly became the narrator for Mike's information-starved friends. It was then that I began to develop my individuality, conveying with drama the happenings of the illustrious Marsh clan.

During my more solemn times of that visit, I noticed the gap widen between Paul, David, and me. While I still felt the occasional urge to erupt and "do something," it was now tempered with a sense of military discipline that helped sustain my impulsive cravings. David, still the lovable goofball, after school worked part time as a plumber's apprentice, then devoted any free time remaining to any classes on plumbing at night school. But it was Paul who worried both David and me. By then Paul seemed more aggravated and withdrawn than ever before. When I discovered he had skipped school the majority of the time—the same school David was attending—part of me wanted to go ballistic and rip him to shreds, but, with hardly a word of concern or disapproval, I'd smile at Paul, hoping in time that things would somehow right themselves. As hard as we tried, David and I could not decipher Paul's enormous life-altering quandary. I only knew that Paul, like most teens his age, had problems getting along with his parents, had missed Michael Marsh terribly, and still craved to perform outlandish feats, yet maybe, like me, Paul simply didn't want to advance to the next level of adulthood and final independence. David and I agreed that whatever Paul's dilemma, it hardly justified the cold, sarcastic, cancerlike chip growing on his shoulder with every passing day. Yet whenever I'd gently probe, Paul would go into his "It's me against the world" routine, and I'd retreat by nodding my head while hoping not to sock him into orbit. Unlike David, who advised and at times berated our friend because he loved him, I never offered the slightest critique against Paul in whom I saw all the limitless opportunities—that he could easily pluck like fruit from a tree and that now were slipping from his grasp. What gnawed most at David and me was that our Einstein, Jr., had opportunities as vast as the stars above, things that David and I could never obtain, but he only seemed to linger in his own mire. But, yet, no matter how Paul was living his life, my affections for him rarely waned. He was still my friend.

I had returned to Duinsmoore many times since then. The most devastating of my visits was days after my biological father—whom I had seen less than a dozen times while in foster care—lost his long bout with cancer of the neck and throat, and who died in my arms without ever stating the three words I had so longed to hear. So it was Duinsmoore I fled to and Dan's support I longed for. After attending Sunday Mass, with Dan kneeling beside me and after having locked away a torrid of mixed emotions for so many years, I broke down in front of Mr. Brazell in his backyard, realizing Dan had provided me with more devotion and guidance in those few years than my own father in his lifetime. Years later when I became a proud father, Dan was one of the first I phoned, and in the months to follow I'd constantly bug him and mail him a small arsenal of photographs of my growing son. In April of 1991 when I returned home from the war in the Gulf, serving as an air crew member—I was a midair refueler for the once-coveted SR-71 Blackbird and the once-mysteriously-shrouded F-117 Stealth Fighter—the Duinsmoore neighborhood converged at Mrs. Howard's home, as I proudly held my five-year-old son, Stephen, in my arms while chatting with Dan. By chance someone snapped a photo of that magical moment. To the casual observer the picture holds nothing special: just a child with wide, glistening, smiling eyes while in the arms of a father sporting a short military crew cut hairstyle, gazing back at a man of respect who places his hand on the shoulder of the young father. I have since dubbed the framed photograph *Three Generations*.

Though many years have passed, David Howard and I continue to remain in constant contact with each other. After running down the usual checklist of the families' status, we spend the majority of our time conversing about Paul and our concerns for his happiness. When time permits, we relive the era of our youth and amplify the exploits, wondering with laughter how we were never arrested, flogged in public by the neighborhood, or didn't end up dead from absolute ignorance. These talks with David, and on my rare conversations with The Sarge, which are as natural as breathing, without any thought or hesitation we'd end our discussions with those three most important words, vowing to talk soon and possibly making plans to see each other in the near future.

THE PRIVILEGE OF YOUTH

Like everyone, I find my life way too busy and, at times, chaotically out of control. I have promised myself dozens upon dozens of times that *this* is the year I will slow down. *This* is the year that I can, that I *must* block off some time and spend a few days with Mike, or have David and his lovely bride, Kelly, come for a visit. I have broken my pledge more times than I can count. And now I am middle-aged and realize I am on the "back nine" of the game called life and am left wondering how many more opportunities I have left.

In all my years and seemingly lifetime of worldly adventures, Duinsmoore Way has been and remains an essential part of my everyday life. With limited mechanical skills, I've applied myself in the area of gardening. Fulfilling a lifetime dream of having lived amongst the redwood trees in Northern California, even if I returned home at two in the morning, after being on the road for well over a month, I'd spring out of bed like a child on Christmas precisely at five o'clock, race downstairs to make a pot of freshly ground coffee, before stepping outside to gaze in awe at the sun rising against the backdrop of a serene transparent Russian River. Then, while sipping my brew, as Dan had done all those years, I, too, surveyed my work area in which I would plant hundreds upon hundreds of bright impatiens flowers in a precise arrangement—which I had blueprinted in my head while on the road—only after toiling the soil. At times whenever neighbors dropped by for a chat, they most likely talked to my backside, but as stoic as I may have appeared, I always greeted everyone with a long, mellow *hellooow*. And, like Dan, I'd apply myself non-stop, wrapping up around three o'clock, initiated by cleaning every tool with a fresh rag, dusting off every shelf, then sweeping out my tiny workshed with my heavy-duty broom, before proudly hosing off the entire driveway.

With work done, and after taking a shower and surveying the task that I always seemed to endlessly critique, I'd become like The Sarge within my small tight-knit condominium community. The core group would either converge by my carport or at "Ray and Rey's" to discuss current events, the state of the Union, unyielding taxes, or some kid down the block who plays his latest hard-core, ballistically angry music, in decibels way too loud, the neighbor who drives down the narrow street at Mach-like speeds, or the guy who turns a blind eye while his thin unkempt dog does his business in other people's yards. To my own shock and horror, I discover that my rants, raves, and rising blood pressure over it all has made me part of *The Establishment*. So, with a bottle of chilled dark Spaten German beer clutched in my hand, I'd hold court to relay my epic travels or offer *my* take on various topics with a patented mishmash of dramatic verbs and colorful adjectives—what the group has become accustomed to as "Pelz-Lang," the phrase for which my lovely wife, Marsha, takes credit for coining. Later in the stillness of the night, after lighting a candled lantern that my mentor Mr. Marsh would have proudly dubbed The Beacon of Hope, on my front porch I'd sit on my faded director's chair and enjoy a Carbonell cigar, conversing with an occasional neighbor out for an evening stroll. Living in the beautiful yet peculiar town of Guerneville—a town often teased by some as "The Home of Third Generation Retired Hippies"—with my condo nestled within the Dubrava complex, an overwhelming sense of pride and camaraderie radiated from nearly everyone within our gated community. For me it was my *mini* Duinsmoore.

But after years of surviving numerous Noah-like floods and enduring Arctic-like winters, my family and I now proudly reside in Southern California, in a spacious two-bedroom home with a garage, within yet another community, where my precious bride, Marsha, and I are the youngest residents by at least twenty-five years. We are also one of the only couples not to flee to cooler climates and a secondary home when the summer barometer simmers over 120 degrees. Because we rarely see each other, Marsha, Stephen, and I keep to ourselves. The only time I see my fellow "Cove members" is when they observe our two Bichon dogs—Titan (aka Big Boy) and Ernie (The Psycho Pup)—who both take *me* for a walk as they desperately try to capture birds in midflight or lizards on the ground. The Palm Springs area heat, coupled with my midage metabolism, prohibits me from indulging too much in my German libation, so my pallet has changed from my beloved Spaten Optimator to an occasional Merlot.

I no longer wander under God's majestic redwood trees, strolling over to a friend's front porch to be part of Dubrava's give-and-take, but have now found refuge within the confines of a local cigar establishment. Days after moving to the Palm Springs area, I staked out the stogie shop located on Coachella Valley's high-end shopping boulevard, which would shame the famed Rodeo Drive in Hollywood. During my first few visits I'd plop down on a wooden bench and tap away on my laptop computer, keeping to myself while working on my latest tome, but occasionally listening to the different cliques that came in to converse. The famed proprietors, Jack and Bert, would kindly allow me to take up space as long as I needed, and over time, like Duinsmoore and Dubrava, I became acquainted with the cadre group. There's Dick, a retired NASA rocket engineer, and "King George," both of whom work at the shop. Others include "Handsome Harry," who visits the area several times a month and whose wife counsels the celebrity types like Jennifer, Brad, Farrah, and Fergie. There's a young entrepreneur dubbed Scotty "Too Hotty" who publishes a sports magazine, and Marshall who bares the striking resemblance and mischievous smile of a towering Mel Gibson. Though the most colorful character has to be that of Wayne—and because of respect and his extensive military background, I address him as "Colonel," for Colonel Wayne has the distinction of being a survivor of the famed Black Hawk helicopter crashes from the special operational mission in Mogadishu, Somalia.

Back at my home office I proudly maintain my aeronautical, historical, and general informational library that would impress even my scholarly mentor, Professor Marsh. Displayed across from the photos of my radiant wife, I proudly keep a collage of those famed photographs of Dan,

Stephen, and me together. Hanging on the side of my wall is a gift from Mike Marsh, the curator of the Marsh Institute of Aeronautical studies—that reads in part:

If where you are going doesn't excite you, getting there will.
Get into it!

And now years later I am still into it. For my adventures are never ending. With all the action, excitement, and chaos my life at times encompasses, I feel fortunate that I am "out there" "doing something" with the time I have left on this planet. The day I moved from Northern to Southern California, the expedition began after being on the road for several weeks, only to take four flights from New Hampshire so to stumble into San Francisco airport just after four in the morning, to make the three-hour drive to Guerneville, secure a U-Haul, load it up, *then* turn around and make the nonstop ten-hour drive to my family's new home. In all, I planned to arrive in the Palm Springs area by eleven that evening. Yet before I could begin my final journey north, within the confines of the beloved Bay Area, I had planned to drive by the house from my childhood in Daly City and offer a prayer. For years, ever since moving to Guerneville, after making hundreds of trips from the redwood-laden town to San Francisco International Airport, I always crept down the quiet street in Daly City, stopping my truck for a moment to reflect while offering a quick prayer that both deceased parents are finally resting in peace and that my brothers are safe and well with their lives and their families.

But before seeing my childhood home, which held bitter-sweet memories for me, I deviated south from the airport via Highway 101 to a more joyful setting. After taking the Marsh road exit onto Bay Road, I slowed down my vehicle and lowered my windows to breathe in the crisp, chilly air. Easing my truck to a crawl within the middle of Duins-moore, it quickly becomes enveloped in a blanket of swirl-ing gray fog. The rustling of the trees never ceases, and the homes within the dark stillness of the night still shine with opulence. I can smell the jasmine as I did a lifetime ago, and for a moment I don't have to rush, worry about how many socks or ties I've packed for my lengthy journey, eventually trying to find my way through my mazelike directions in the middle of the night, struggling to find a small town that doesn't even exist on the map, and deal with the pressure I put on myself so I can do well in whatever my task. For a brief moment of time I am back at Duinsmoore, I am free to play as long and as hard as I desire, free of all anxiety that only adults place upon themselves. For now I have all the time of day that the sun's brilliance can offer. I can almost picture the street teeming with children, the sounds of their giggling innocence echoing in every direction, while a herd of men converge at Dan's garage.

A sense of calm fills me. In a blink of an eye, I envision with perfect clarity the time I paid my final respects to Mr. Brazell. With only a small window of time and cursing my-self that I was unable to cancel a program that had been booked for well over a year in advance, I flew into the Bay Area from back east only to step back on another wide-body jet in a matter of hours, thus making me unable to attend Dan's services. Instead, Marsha, my fiancée at the time, and I attended the evening Rosary in the same pew Dan and I used to find solace. On my knees I kept my strained emotions under control, while casting an occasional eye on Dan's family in the front right pew. Afterward, Marsha and I greeted the Brazell family outside to offer our deepest condolences. Then, in an adjoining room, Marsha and I milled like lost sheep among the throng in awkward silence, glancing down at our shoes until someone burst out with the idea of a group photo, like those from the ol' neighborhood. By reflex, I immediately bowed my head down as I led Marsha and myself away, yet some soft unknown hand took mine, guiding me back within the group. I stood tall by the Neyland and Howard families, as well as folks I have not seen or thought about in years. After adjusting ourselves for the paparazzi of photographers, I nudged up to a sweaty Mr. Jolly and a tall, radiant, grown-up Amy Neyland. For one of life's precious, unforgettable moments before anyone captures the scene on film, all of us turn our heads, staring in one another's faces, nodding and smiling, communicating a message without the need of mere words, knowing full well the unique bond between us all. Before a set of cameras flash, someone commands, "Leave a space for Dan!" On the count of three, everyone shouts, "To Dan!" And, like everyone else, I can feel Mr. Brazell's presence standing tall beside me.

It is then I realize it took me twenty years, but I had finally made it to Duinsmoore.

ACKNOWLEDGMENTS

As always, this project could have not been accomplished, let alone have maintained the standards set by the preceding books without Marsha Pelzer's invaluable editing services. After years of marriage, working together, and our heated "disagreements," you always decoded my Pelzisms, knowing what I am trying to convey, even when I don't exactly write what I think I mean.

My agent and good friend Laurie Liss for all your trust, care, and allowing me to bombard you anytime and place when your assistance, your voice, or wicked sense of humor was needed. Laurie, you truly are the best of the best.

Rey Thayne, Office Manager Extraordinaire for your valuable time, patience, and courtesy; keeping me on track when my life runs awry; but most of all your trust. Thanks, Rey, for all the work you've accomplished to help others in need.

Amanda Lukowski, for planning my travel with military-like precision and flawlessness for nearly ten years. Your work frees me to focus on doing the best job possible when I'm "out there." This acknowledgment is long overdue and for that, Amanda, I apologize.

ACKNOWLEDGMENTS

To my publishing family at Dutton: This project was the least painful of them all, for all of us. So, kudos to Vice President and Editorial Director (pretty fancy title, eh?) Extraordinaire and good friend, Brian Tart. Amy Hughes, for her time and laughs. Brant Janeway at the PR department for all your time, and, most important, your confidence.

A special acknowledgment to the institutions: to Palm Desert Tobacco, where billows of fine cigar smoke float freely throughout its confines, allowing all who partake in one of the last great freedoms of a democratic society. And to Sullivan's Steak House where great food, live jazz, and the adult libation known as the Dave-tini are always the order of the day. Thank you both for allowing me to plug-in, type away, and take up space in the midst of your businesses. I am truly, truly appreciative.

And, a special thank-you to you the reader. By nature, writing is a lonely profession. Most of my writing is "attempted" at airport terminals at four in the morning; in bathroom stalls; darkened, dingy, smoke-filled lounges; moldy motel lobbies. Or the writing is frantic notes scribbled against the steering wheel while driving at high speeds searching for the one word, that single phrase that might, just might, lead to a good sentence, or a good scene that will make all the difference in capturing that spirit, grabbing someone's heart, or taking them back to a place they have not been to in such a long time. You, the reader, make the story great. Without your time and compassion to the craft, I am but a person scribing on a black chalkboard with a black piece of chalk.

Duinsmoore Way
Perspective

DAVID HOWARD

Menlo Park has always been a slightly upscale, old, small bedroom community with an even smaller housing track that boasts the longest standing homeowner's association in northern California. Within this microcommunity is Suburban Park. I lived on one of the most popular blocks in the association called Duinsmoore Way. Duinsmoore was at the center of Suburban Park and its activities. Here lived some of the most inspirational and talented people in my life, one of whom was David Pelzer. Before I tell you about David, you need to know more about how I had met David.

While I lived at the third house south of the corner, my good friend Paul Brazell lived across the street and two doors down, and the Marsh family lived across the street from Paul. Next door to the Marshes was a house that was the talk of the neighboorhood. It was a rental house, which was uncommon here, and where foster kids lived! Some of my early recollections of the kids in this house were that they always looked and acted older than they were. I was warned not to talk to them, as they were unscrupulous thugs with long criminal records and were outcasts from society. I believed what I was told, due in part to the fact that none of the kids stayed long and they all kept to themselves. . . . That is, until David.

I met David in the fall of 1975 while I was practicing for a not-too-promising basketball career. David walked by several times before I asked him if he wanted to play. He said he was not very good at basketball, and to my surprise I discovered someone even worse than me.

Later that day I was riding down the block on my bike when a voice called out to me. I turned and, to my astonishment, it was David, and he was working on his minibike in the driveway of the foster kids' house. I didn't know what to do. Do I go over and talk to him, or ignore him in the hopes he will go away? I took a chance and went over to talk to him. I could feel the heavy stares of the neighborhood on my back. Shortly after talking to David, Paul came over and we all became friends.

David was a few years older than me. He was skinny, wore glasses, and was unsure of his physical actions, which made people look at him as clumsy and uncoordinated. David was not what the community of neighbors thought he was. He was an individual with a strong desire to fit in and a need to have close friends. Even then, and more so to this very day, David was a loyal and trustworthy friend, always with enough time to spend listening to your prob-

214

lems and doing whatever he could to help make anyone happy.

As a kid, David didn't have a lot of personal items, but the ones he did have were so very precious to him. When I was little, at Christmastime, all the kids on the block would be showered with presents to the point of gluttony. That is, everyone but David. I remember one Christmas when Paul and I met up with David and talked about all the presents we had received. Thinking back now, I can't remember even one of the presents that either Paul or I had received that year, yet I remember all of David's. He received a worn, cheap, oversized vinyl jacket; a Cox model airplane; and a boom box. Later I witnessed a gang of about nine older kids from the other side of town trying to take his radio away from him. After seeing David being beaten, kicked, and pummeled by the entire gang and never giving up, I realized the magnitude of the torture he must have endured. He fought back as if his life depended on keeping his Christmas presents, while the gang kept hitting him and hitting him. He showed no fear, but I could not say the same.

Once when I reluctantly went to David's foster home, I was shocked to find David's room consisted of a bed and a dresser, with no items in view. His sparse closet had a dozen or so hangers with shirts and pants neatly arranged on the hangers. His bedroom was a room without feeling or substance, reminding me of a motel room where you know you are going to stay the night, yet you still do not unpack fully. Excluding his minibike, David could pack all his worldly possessions in a small suitcase, located under his bed, and still have room to spare.

It took time and a little maturity on my part to grasp why David loved Duinsmoore as much as he did. The three of us had a lot of fun growing up in this small community. In time, most of the people on the block warmed to David's presence and allowed him access into their lives. There are some exceptions who, even today and after all of David's fame and accomplishments, will still bolt their doors when he comes to visit. The crazy and sometimes almost illegal stunts that most adolescents perform in their campaign toward adulthood seemed to have been on steroids when we preformed them. The endless hours of discussions, not only of the day's harrowing experiences but also of the life we intended to pursue, only led to the career choices we tried to make. I thought of being a fireman or policeman, Paul a race-car mechanic or Airborne Ranger just like our high-spirited neighbor Mike Marsh. David's longing was a combination of everything, just as long as he never became homeless. While Paul became an auto mechanic, I had started toward my career as a public servant when an opportunity to become a plumber diverted my career path. In time, David received his Jump Wings through Army Airborne training, flew around the world in James Bond–like top-secret missions for the United States Air Force, counseled troubled youth in juvenile hall, and has literally accomplished so much of which I am extremely proud.

The time the three of us shared seemed to last forever.

For David in particular, every minute of every hour was precious to him. I realized the full impact of David's appreciation when one day I was walking over to David's foster home and saw a strange car sitting in his front yard. There stood David next to the car, his well-traveled suitcase in hand. I asked him where he was going and he simply, coldly said, "Away." When prompted, he stated that he was being transferred to another home, but that he was probably going to juvenile hall until a new home was found. In an instant, he was gone. I will never forget that empty feeling in the pit of my stomach, watching my friend disappear to Lord-knows-where and wondering if I would ever see David again.

Like all young men who aspire, Paul, David, and I grew, worked, and ventured in separate ways. Marriage, children, careers, and everyday life left little time for us to get together. The phone calls became fewer and farther between, as did the visits. It seems that the older a person becomes, the days get shorter and time seems to speed by, leaving less time to keep in contact with good friends to revisit those days of wonder.

To this day, Paul is closely associated with Duinsmoore, and I am too, especially when my beloved elderly mother calls in the wee hours of the morning, terrified of a raccoon that has somehow burrowed under her house. David, too, still carries Duinsmoore close to his heart. When our dear friend Dan Brazell was still with us, David used to make the several-hour drive to see him on Father's Day, and for years now it has become a tradition for my mother and other mothers within the Duinsmoore community to receive an intimidating-sized bouquet of flowers from David on Mother's Day. And now, with David's *Privilege of Youth*, Duinsmoore Way will forever be immortalized as a community that meant so much to so many, especially to my friend David.

I will always miss David and the times we had in our adolescence. I consider David to be my brother and my best friend. The memories of my childhood are filled with love and adventure. Before Duinsmoore, I had often wondered what David's were full of.

Duinsmoore Way
Perspective

Michael Marsh

Suburban Park was a quiet, unpretentious bedroom community in Menlo Park on what is known as The Peninsula, which extends south to San Jose from San Francisco. It was where my family and I lived in our first home, from 1970 to 1979 when we moved to Denver, Colorado. The 100-block of Duinsmoore Way was a street that was occupied by a potpourri of families who truly represented a cross-sectional slice of Americana. Farnham, Neylan, Ferrara, Marsh, Brazell, Jolly, Howard, and Beaulaurier were all families who interacted, socialized, played, celebrated, and supported one another, and were all families on a street that David Pelzer adopted—against some of their wishes.

Duinsmoore Way was quiet most of the year, but on at least three occasions a year it was alive with the sounds of rock bands, street parties, and fireworks, most of which were in the distinctly illegal category. At the ripe age of thirty, and as a surviving combatant of the Vietnam War, I was, or fancied myself to be, something of a *bon vivant*.

Therefore, for at least two or three years, I hosted a birthday party on March 21, featuring beer kegs and a rock band. It was called "Spring Rites" by my friends and neighbors, and it was a rigorous affair, enthusiastically attended by friends, neighbors, and occasional passersby. Then one year, my patient but practical then-wife announced an end to Spring Rites. It was fun while it lasted, but it had been in danger of getting out of hand. The Duinsmoore Street Party evolved from the annual Suburban Park Association Picnic, which had been held for many years at Flood Park, but died because the neighborhood was bored and wanted something livelier. I had been cajoled into becoming president of the Suburban Park Association, and the board figured out we could have a DJ, an inflatable jumping castle, booths, etc., and the Street Party was born. The third event of the year that every neighborhood dog dreaded was the Fourth of July, and it was a major-league shoot-out, which of course today would be punishable by all the Health & Safety Fascists, The No Fun Allowed League, and Seriousness Police. It was closely supervised with adult garden-hose quick-response teams and one helluva lot of really, really fine illegal fireworks. I'll never forget a largeish rocket gone astray, exploding under Gary ("G. Jolly from Cal-Poly") Jolly's lawn chair as he observed the pyrotechnics. The next day everybody manned brooms and rakes to clean the street and yards.

On my fiftieth birthday (several years ago, now) I was presented with a book full of letters from well-wishers, and several of my nieces and nephews had written testimonials on how, as children, they had been witness to unbelievable displays of fireworks at Uncle Mike's house on the Fourth of July. As a great admirer of Mark Twain, I can only remark that our lawless behavior way back then was elegant in its innocence.

It was this eclectic, tiny corner of American society that David Pelzer happened into, and whether you believe it was fate, providence, God, or just plain luck (good or bad), it had a catalyzing effect on his dim, naive, and limited perception of life, future, and opportunity. My across-the-street neighbor, the late Dan Brazell, was a fair and honest man who wanted Dave to be something more than a loser. Dan and I spent a good amount of time ragging, nagging, hassling, and antagonizing Dave, primarily because Dave needed it. In today's politically-correct society this wouldn't be deemed appropriate, but Dave turned out to be something other than a loser. He became a winner. That wasn't because of Dan Brazell or me or Duinsmoore Way; it was because Dave determined what he would be. Mark Twain might sum it up thusly: *"He was a no good lout; a failure so miserable everyone loathed his success and admired his achievements."*

—Michael Marsh, curator of the Marsh Institute of
Advanced Aeronautical Studies, Lakewood, CO

Duinsmoore Way
Perspective

Mrs. Howard

Please understand, I am not the gushy type. I have a hard time expressing feelings. So, this is how I feel:

I am the blessed mother of two extraordinary children, David and Cheryl. But through a seemingly ordinary occurrence, I came to know and love an extremely haggard young child whom I have called my "other son."

When David Pelzer first moved into our neighborhood as a foster child, I must admit it raised more than a few eyebrows. At the time, I knew very little about foster care and even less about David's past, but one could clearly see this young man could overcome anything.

I've always prided myself on raising my two children to not be smug or judgmental but rather tolerant and kind— to walk a mile in the shoes of others before being critical. David Pelzer had wandered through the depths of hell before being saved and tempered in waters of love, family, and community that he held so dear.

When my son, David, first introduced David Pelzer to

our family, he seemed more like a shy, quiet animal ready to bolt at the slightest movement or sound. Whenever a voice was raised, his hands would literally shake. His eyes were intense, as was his attention, which never wavered. To David Pelzer, everything held a certain significance. Whether it was cookies I had just baked for the stream of children who went to and fro in our house, or chocolate cheesecake that David would slice ever so slowly and razor-thin so it would melt in his mouth before he could savor a taste, or an off-the-cuff compliment that he would absorb like a sponge, this young boy held everything as if it were gold.

David Pelzer was also pure of heart. Not only did he carry a deep sense of compassion that made him wise and mature well beyond his years, but what struck me, my family, and even those who were overly leery of the presence of a foster child within Duinsmoore, was David's sincerity, gratitude, and respect toward everyone he came in contact with. As clumsy and withdrawn as he appeared to be, David would practically kill "The Duinsmoore Crowd" with a courteous respectful "Yes, sir" or "No, ma'am" whenever addressed. Even for the hardcore "Crowd," David's manner made them take notice of this young man's potential.

At times, when my son, David, and my "other son" resembled Tom Sawyer and Huckleberry Finn with their rambunctious adventures, David Pelzer's persistence in bettering himself while keeping a genuinely kind attitude propelled him into a league that few have joined, or ever will. He was the type of person who gave everything he had to everything he did, while offering a wave rather than looking for a handout. All he needed was a little love and a hug.

To this day, whenever in the Bay Area and no matter how tired or how long his travels take him, David drops by. Every Mother's Day without fail, my "other son" adorns me with a bouquet of roses that are beyond belief. Above his acts of kindness and generosity in his cause of helping others, David Pelzer's proudest achievement is his son, who, like his father, is a kind, sincere young man who is coming into his own, too.

While David Pelzer gives much credit of his success to families such as the Brazells, the Marshes, and mine, if indeed those days of Duinsmoore made a difference in David's young life, I am both flattered and proud beyond words. To some, Duinsmoore is nothing more than a quaint little neighborhood. To my three children, the impact of Duinsmoore enabled me to nurture and care for them as any parent should, so that when they became of age, they, too, could live a life filled with love and happiness.

ABOUT THE AUTHOR

A former air force aircrew member, Dave proudly served in the USAF for more than thirteen years. He played a major role in Operations Just Cause, Desert Shield, and Desert Storm. Dave was selected for the unique task of midair refueling of the once highly secretive SR-71 Blackbird and the F-117 Stealth Fighter. While serving in the air force, Dave worked in juvenile hall and other programs involving "youth-at-risk" throughout California.

Dave's exceptional accomplishments include commendations from Presidents Reagan, Bush, Clinton, and George W. Bush, as well as other various heads of state. While maintaining an international active-duty fight schedule, Dave was the recipient of the 1990 JCPenney Golden Rule Award, making him the California Volunteer of the Year. In 1993, Dave was honored as one of the Ten Outstanding Young Americans (TOYA), joining a distinguished group of alumni that includes Chuck Yeager, Christopher Reeve, Anne Bancroft, John F. Kennedy, Orson Welles, and Walt Disney. In

1994, Dave was the *only* American to be selected as one of The Outstanding Young Persons of the World (TOYP) for his efforts involving child-abuse awareness and prevention, as well as for promoting resilience and self-responsibility in others. During the Centennial Olympic Games, Dave was a torchbearer, carrying the coveted flame.

Dave is the author of four other inspirational books: *A Child Called "It,"* which has been on the *New York Times* bestseller list for more than five years; *The Lost Boy,* which has been on the same list for more than four years; and *A Man Named Dave,* a bestseller for nearly two years. Dave's latest book, *Help Yourself,* was also an instant *New York Times* bestseller. Dave's books have been on the bestseller list for more than eleven years combined.

Dave is currently at work on his next book, which deals with issues for teens, entitled *Help Yourself for Teens.* His future works may include a tome entitled *My Wife's Life: One Husband's Quest to Understand the Complexities of the Married Female Psyche.*

When not on the road with his wife, Marsha, or son, Stephen, or submitting to his recent addiction to golf, Dave lives a quiet life in Southern California with his two Bichon dogs, Titan ("Big Boy") and Ernie ("the Psycho Pup") and his box turtle named Chuck.

For more information you can visit Dave's Web site at www.davepelzer.com.